ONE IN A MILLION

ONE IN
A MILLION

The story of Billy Graham's missions
in England during 1984

Derek Williams

WORD BOOKS (UK) LTD
NORTHBRIDGE ROAD, BERKHAMSTED

ISBN 0 85009 054 7

Photographs by: Russ Busby, Clive Heaphy and Bill Spencer
Cover and colour section designed by: Barbara Pontes

Design, phototypesetting and production by
Nuprint Services Ltd, Harpenden, Herts AL5 4SE

Printed in Great Britain for
WORD BOOKS (UK) LTD
Northbridge Road, Berkhamsted, Herts HP4 1EH by
Purnell & Sons (Book Production) Ltd, Paulton, Bristol BS18 5LQ

Contents

To the many whose names are not recorded here, but are written in the Book of Life as a result of the Billy Graham missions in England in 1984. Yours shall be the greater reward; 'for there is nothing hidden that will not be disclosed.'

Introduction

The summer of '84

It was quite a summer in 1984. Britain slowly dried up under rainless skies, giving scant sympathy to Ethiopians suffering a far more terrifying drought, while the clouds of bitterness and anger thickened over the personalities involved in the seemingly endless coal miners' strike.

The British people once again demonstrated their island independence by staying away in great numbers from the European elections. In South Africa a majority of 'coloureds' boycotted the elections which gave them a vote for the first time but which many saw as only a cosmetic change to apartheid policy. In India, several dozen Sikh militants, anxious for greater political recognition, died inside their holy shrine, the Golden Temple of Amritsar, after a gun battle.

A new Bishop of Durham, one of the senior clergy in the Church of England, was finally enthroned in his Cathedral after surviving protests about his denial of the traditional doctrines of the virgin birth and the resurrection. The roof of York Minster was gutted by fire after being hit by a lightning bolt (some said as a result of the Durham appointment), while north of the border the Church of Scotland General Assembly decided that there was no biblical justification for calling God 'Our Mother', and that the traditional formulation of the Lord's Prayer should remain unchanged.

And sandwiched between the London Marathon in June

and the opening of the Los Angeles Olympics in August, during which time John McEnroe again won the Wimbledon tennis championship and England's cricketers repeatedly collapsed before the pace attack of their West Indian visitors, there was an event which often made Britain's regional headlines but which may prove in time to have been of national significance.

American evangelist Billy Graham embarked, at 65 years of age, on his most intensive mission (the American word 'crusade' was studiously avoided for reasons which will become clear later) for two decades, and saw it produce statistical results beyond his, and the organisers', wildest dreams.

During May, June and July he preached at 41 meetings divided between six soccer grounds from Bristol in the South West to Sunderland in the North East, taking in Birmingham in the Midlands, Liverpool in the North West, and Norwich and Ipswich in East Anglia. The attendance topped a million, and on a few occasions the stadium gates were locked before the start of the meetings and latecomers had to watch the proceedings on large-screen TV in a nearby park.

Almost 100,000 people 'went forward' at the end of the meetings as a public sign of their new commitment to Christ, and to seek further spiritual counsel. They represented 9.4 per cent of the attendance, which was twice the proportion normally seen at Graham missions in other parts of the world. One of the highest responses on record anywhere, 14.5 per cent, was seen on a damp night in what had previously been dubbed 'the graveyard of evangelists', Sunderland.

The missions drew such intense local media interest that nearly half the requests for interviews had to be turned down through sheer lack of time. Some 50,000 column inches of news and features about the missions were printed in national and regional papers, and over 13 hours of radio and TV coverage was given (all, of course, at the companies' initiative and expense as air time cannot be bought in Britain, unlike the USA).

What was perhaps more significant was the total of 5,000 churches of all denominations which found a new unity by actively working together for the missions, and many more sent coachloads of people to the meetings. Nearly 50,000 church members went through a training class to help them understand and share their faith more effectively, and as a result many people discovered gifts and ministries they did not know they had.

For Billy Graham's three month tour was only a part – even though the central part – of a three year programme of local church training and outreach known as Mission England. In 1983, churches were encouraged to re-examine their priorities and to train their members for witness, out-reach, and caring for new Christians. In 1984, Billy Graham's visit provided the focus for active evangelism. In 1985, the evangelism was to continue, building on the contacts made locally with smaller scale and church-based activities.

This book is the story of that central phase, but it sets the missions in their proper context of the three-year programme, which, at the time of writing, is not yet over. It cannot, unfortunately, tell everything, mention every person, recount every anecdote. That would fill an encyclopaedia and take eternity to write. For simplicity's sake, I have taken themes and specific examples, even in chapters on individual regions, rather than endlessly repeat similar details. Nor can it attempt to analyse at any depth the results of the missions because it is too close in time to them. But the news from the missions is too good to keep within the filing cabinets of regional offices and the memories of those closest to the action. It deserves to be told, and pondered.

For some months before the Graham tour, and for the tour itself, it was my privilege to be close to the action as a member of the Mission England/Billy Graham press team. That inevitably smacks of biased reporting, although it had the great advantage of giving me access to minutes of meet-ings and to key personnel, and insight into the backstage 'creative struggles' which began with disagreement and ended (usually) in unity. They have not been swept under the carpet here, even if they are largely overshadowed by the events themselves.

It would be wrong, though, to hide my immense gratitude for having been able to work alongside a dedicated team of highly professional people; for once, Christian work was not allowed to suffer much from amateur blundering. Nor shall I forget the sheer fun of it. Being driven in cars by Americans who could never understand the British rule about giving way to the right at roundabouts (they call them traffic circles), and introducing them to the English art of eating fish and chips out of newspaper on a draughty Northumbrian beach, will for ever remain in my memory.

So too will the fact that while I was at the farthest end of the country my wife shouldered the task of selling our house and buying another which I had not even seen. Fortunately, our tastes are similar. My small children coped with my prolonged and hard-to-explain absences 'working with Billy Graham' by inventing a new, benign mythical figure for their fantasy games.

'I'm a robot!'

'I'm a Billigum.'

Which, in an odd sort of way, brings me to the enigmatic title of this book. It is not about numbers (I have already given you most of them), nor is it a celebration of organisation. Rather, it is about the ones and the twos: the people who gave up jobs and time to help reach others with the gospel of Jesus Christ; the people who made up that total of 100,000 enquirers but who found in some quite unique way that Billy Graham had a message for them personally.

(The names of some counsellors, and the enquirers they talked to, are fictitious, but their stories are quite true. To preserve the confidence of the counselling system I have given only a (false) Christian name to such people. In referring to others by their real names, I have used *both* Christian and surnames (even for Billy Graham!) to distinguish them clearly.)

So this is the story of the ones who made up the million. People like George and Margaret, for example...

I

By special arrangement

George and Margaret still cannot explain how it happened. They were counsellors at the Billy Graham meetings in Bristol. Their 17 year old daughter, Judith, was in the choir.

One evening, as usual, the couple went down onto the Ashton Gate football field at the end of the meeting to talk and pray with people who had come forward as a public act of commitment to Christ. Their task finished, they rejoined a friend they had brought with them. They left the stadium, walked the short distance to the workers' car park, and drove the few miles home.

They opened the front door about ten o'clock. The phone was ringing.

'Dad? It's Judith here. What's happening? Where did you get to? I'm still at the stadium.'

George and Margaret were transfixed for a moment. How could they have totally forgotten their teenage daughter who had ridden with them to the meeting? George got back into the car.

Noticing that the fuel gauge was low, he called into one of the few filling stations still open at that time of night. It was not the one he normally used.

As he worked the pump, he realised that he was still wearing his rather conspicuous blue and white counsellor's badge. Thinking it would look odd, so far from the stadium, he began to unpin it, but some inner prompting made him change his mind. It was still on his coat as he went to pay. The girl at the cash desk noticed it.

'I'd have liked to have heard Billy Graham,' she said, a little wistfully. 'But I'm working every week night.'

'What about Saturday?' asked George.

'I'm not working then. But I haven't got any transport to get me there.' The girl, Wendy, was in her twenties, and pregnant.

'I'm going with my family on a bus from our church,' said George. 'We could meet you and all go down together.'

'Thanks. I'd like that.' Wendy smiled.

Judith, her feet and hands cold from their unexpectedly long exposure to the fresh spring air, eventually fell gratefully into her father's car and was sped home through the dark streets. She was one of four children. Sandra, her 21 year old sister, had been resisting all suggestions that she should join the family outings to Ashton Gate; although a Christian, her faith had ebbed. On the Friday of that week, however, she watched a TV news report of the meetings. Suddenly, she decided that she, too, should go to hear Billy Graham the next day. Mark, the ten year old junior of the family, also planned to go.

So it was a somewhat enlarged group which set off to join 38,000 others at Billy Graham's last meeting in Bristol. They heard him preach on the second coming of Christ.

'The world system which is dominated by evil will come to an end,' he asserted. '"Thy kingdom come" is a prayer that has not yet been answered.'

Before Christ returns there will be false messiahs, he said. He had even had people claiming to be Christ turn up on his own doorstep. But when the real Jesus does come, people will be judged, nature will be changed, and the world will be made a safe place once again.

He threw out a challenge. 'Are you ready for Jesus? The moment you die will be the end of the world for you.' And then he gave his usual invitation for people to get up out of their seats and make their way to the front as a public demonstration of their determination to accept and follow Christ.

Ten year old Mark turned to Sandra, his big sister. 'I want to go. Will you come down with me?'

She hesitated, then agreed. They got up.

Wendy had also been hesitating. She thought her husband would laugh at her if she returned home a new-born Christian. But seeing Sandra and Mark get up gave her the extra courage she needed; she could go with them. Wendy, too, stepped out into a new phase of her spiritual life.

If: George and Margaret had not forgotten Judith; the car had not needed fuel; George had taken his badge off; there had not been a TV report that Friday; Sandra had not changed her mind; she had refused to go forward with Mark...Wendy would not have made it to the meeting, and to the front. Her husband did not, in fact laugh at her. He too began to think about Christianity.

That chain of events seems a chance in a million. But to George and Margaret it was no accident. It showed them that God was busy with his special arrangements, doing extraordinary things in ordinary people's lives. Others were to come to the same conclusion, although in quite different circumstances.

A perfect match

Somewhere in that same crowd on the final Saturday night at Ashton Gate, Bristol, was another couple, Arthur and Vera. They had never had any interest in the church. Not, that is, until they visited Australia. There they happened to see a weekly religious TV programme featuring well-known American preacher Robert Schuller. Something about the programme gripped them, and they never missed it while they were down under.

On returning to the west country, they began to talk over the implications of Christianity. All around them on hoardings and bus sides were huge red and black posters: *BILLY GRAHAM – worth listening to*. They decided to hear him.

That night, Billy Graham broke with a loose tradition and invited one of the platform guests to come to the microphone and give a word of greeting. To Arthur and Vera's intense surprise, the visitor was Robert Schuller. A minor courtesy on the platform became a major sign to them that God's eye for detail had them in focus.

A hundred miles northwards, and six weeks later, Selina was decidedly nervous. She was a counsellor at Villa Park, Birmingham; she had never done that sort of thing before.

Selina was born in Finland, but had settled in Britain and married an Englishman. Out on the pitch after the meeting, she found herself standing next to a woman who looked roughly her age. She opened up the conversation, and found that the enquirer came from Italy. She had come to England in 1971, the same year as Selina, and had married an Englishman. Despite her Christian background, she had drifted from God for a number of years, an experience which Selina also had once been through.

'This to me confirmed the Lord's perfect guidance,' she said later. 'I was able to identify with this lady from the beginning. I knew I was in the right place and any worries over counselling for the first time in my life just faded away. What wonderful love and care from our Lord!'

No committee of well-intentioned planners, no top-flight administrators equipped with computers, could have matched up these and many similar encounters so perfectly. There was the enquirer who, in a crowd of over 5,000 (counting both enquirers and counsellors) happened to be counselled by the woman who a few weeks before had visited her street and unsuccessfully offered her literature about the mission. There were the two children who recognised their counsellor as a former neighbour, while their mother was up in the stands praying that they would be helped by someone they knew. And there was the person who had previously worked in a psychiatric unit, who on two successive nights counselled people she had known as patients.

Of course, coincidence, like nature, is no final proof of the existence of God. Nor, indeed, can it always be assumed to be a mark of his blessing. The frequent occurrence of such stories during the six missions, however, was seen by many people involved in them as confirmation that the planning, preparing and praying in their small corner was part of something much larger. As Gavin Reid, Mission England's National Director, put it, 'We seemed to have stumbled on a piece of God's agenda.'

It also puts the £1.5 million project, the 1,026,600 attendance and the 96,982 people going forward into proper perspective. Neither the early preparation nor the eventual preaching was geared to an amorphous and anonymous mass. It was geared to people.

'You have two sets of ears,' Billy Graham often said at the meetings. 'Your physical ears will hear my voice. But you will also hear the voice of God speaking inside you, through your 'spiritual ears', as if you were the only person in this stadium.'

And so it often seemed.

Another voice

Jean was invited to go with a friend to the mission at Liverpool's Anfield football ground. She had no idea why she accepted the invitation, but deep inside she knew she should.

As Billy Graham was drawing to a close that night, 'another voice definitely spoke to me the exact words which Dr Graham then repeated,' she reported later. 'All I could say was, "Yes Lord, that's what I want. I want you in my life."'

Lionel, a Jew, also went to one of the Anfield meetings. That night, Billy Graham spoke of the evil which existed in men like Adolf Hitler. He went on to recount, almost as an aside, a visit he had once made to the site of Auschwitz, the concentration camp where many Jews suffered and died. He had gone to lay a wreath and make a speech, but for a while, he said, only the tears, not the words, flowed from him.

Those comments touched Lionel more profoundly than anything else that night, and he went forward to give his life to Christ.

Then there was Sam, an artist in his spare time. Up in

north-east England he had, for the previous six months, painted half a dozen studies of the crucifixion of Jesus. He was fascinated by the subject yet lacked any conscious reason for portraying it. But the night Sam went to hear Billy Graham at Roker Park, Sunderland, the evangelist explained how God forgives people's sins through Jesus' death on the cross.

Sam's pictures suddenly came alive to him. The significance of the cross became personal where before it had been only historical and symbolic. He, too, went forward as a public demonstration of his desire to seek God's forgiveness and to start a new life with the risen Christ.

There was no request box outside the stadium where people's needs, scribbled down on scraps of paper, could be dropped, in the hope that they would be among the lucky few randomly drawn in a spiritual lottery for a mention by the speaker. Many people, of course, made their requests known to God through their prayers. Others, like Sam, perhaps, or Lionel, were not at all sure what their needs were when they set out to hear Billy Graham. The special arrangements were more supernatural than natural; a fulfilment of Jesus' promise: 'God knows what you need before you ask him.'

The common thread in all these human stories is the series of meetings arranged as part of Mission England. They provided a unique opportunity for people to hear the simple proclamation of the basic Christian message in a setting uncluttered by denominational tradition and big enough for the suspicious or the sceptical to feel comfortably anonymous: a soccer ground. Each meeting followed a similar pattern, although each had its own special character, rather like apparently identical hand-knitted jumpers which are never in fact quite the same.

Not everyone who came knew what to expect. As they squeezed through the narrow turnstiles, built for slim youths rather than stout ladies (there were plenty of both at all the meetings), and were shown to their seats by the stewards, this is what they saw and heard, with local variations on the same theme...

2

One night in July

It is ten minutes before eight on a warm, sunny Thursday evening in July 1984. Many of the 32,000 people packed into Liverpool's Anfield football ground are fanning their faces with their magenta tinted programmes. The narrow rows of hard wooden seats offer no space for stretching stiff limbs. On the shallow terraces of the famous Kop – a huge shelter at one end capable of holding over 15,000 people – only thin, flat plastic cushions come between flesh and concrete.

But despite the heat and the cramp, the crowd seems even more responsive than usual; an almost tangible friendliness moulds this mass of humanity – equivalent to the population of a modest town – into a unity. British gospel singer and songwriter Graham Kendrick is quick to sense it.

'Wow! You're lively tonight!' he exclaims after a lusty rendering of *This is the day*. He moves up a gear, leading the crowd through ten minutes of chorus and hymn singing more firmly yet still keeping his gentle, conversational tone. The crowd responds with even greater zest and the concrete and cast iron stands reverberate with the triumphant acclamation, *Our God reigns!* Almost under the cover of the sound, Billy Graham walks along the track to the platform, greeted only by a ripple of applause from the choir which has the closest view of his entrance.

Throughout the missions (except Birmingham, where Dave

Pope deputised) Graham Kendrick has had the job of turning people's thoughts towards God in a place where they would be more naturally hungry for goals.

Anfield, in many respects the Mecca of English soccer, has become for a week a truly holy ground, the venue for the fifth of Billy Graham's six regional missions. The bright, fresh grass is largely covered by almost 30,000 square feet of brown and maroon protective matting. The tightly-packed young shoots are not yet firm enough to withstand unaided a pounding from thousands of feet; they will be punished enough by a weekly onslaught of studded boots sliding mercilessly across the pitch when the soccer season opens in a month's time.

Despite the close attention of anxious stewards, some of them carrying two way radios, small children can still be seen occasionally squatting on the edge of the matting, pulling it back just enough to pluck a blade or two from the hallowed turf, to be smuggled home and given pride of place alongside the team photos and red and white scarves adorning their bedroom walls.

All the usual accoutrements of a soccer match are missing. Instead of eight-foot high goalposts at each end, the focus of attention is a single eight foot high platform in the middle of the pitch, reaching from one touchline to almost where the centre circle would be. Its scaffold undergirding is tastefully draped in royal blue fabric, and leafy pink and yellow flowers sprout from boxes along the front and sides. There are flowers, too, in triangular white boxes in each corner of the field, where on soccer afternoons marker flags would flutter.

The advertising boards have been taken down from the perimeter walls and stand roofs, except the one belonging to the team's sponsors, Crown Paints. Only large banners – 'Jesus said, "I am the way, the truth and the life"' and similar biblical texts – give wandering eyes something to read. There is hardly a policeman's helmet to be seen; the scent of cigarette smoke is much diluted; and the refreshment kiosks are doing only a slow trade in tea and soft drinks.

But that jovial, almost carnival atmosphere remains. If

Anfield has become, as some have claimed, an open air cathedral, then it knows nothing of the cavernous echoes and colourful but quiet rituals which respectively characterise the city's famous Anglican and Roman Catholic cathedrals dominating the skyline a couple of miles away.

For some church leaders here tonight – and many have come – the crowded Anfield scene must provide food for thought. Many half empty and decaying church buildings haunt the inner city wastes and sprawling modern estates of this, one of Britain's most depressed areas. Here, perhaps, is living proof that architecture, or the lack of it, is one of several factors in evangelism. The neutral ground (even to an Everton supporter) is less daunting than the narrow confines of a traditional church. Where there is less apprehension there is more responsiveness and rapport – and greater openness to the message of the meeting.

Of course, there are other factors which help to generate this genial atmosphere. Billy Graham, whose smiling, fatherly face has been beaming down from huge posters plastered around the city for a month, is a media figure who attracts the idly curious who would never cross the threshold of a local church unless they were carried there in a box. You can see them hunched on the Kop terraces, looking slightly detached, and perched on seats in the stands, passing comments and sandwiches to their friends.

No wonder he often begins his addresses with a disclaimer. 'We've not come here to put on a show. We're not here to entertain you. We've come here to see if the Bible has something to say to us today.' It is easy to be a spectator sitting in judgment on a superstar; but the files are already full of stories of people who came to such meetings to experience an event, and went home having had an encounter with God. Meanwhile, curiosity calms the nerves.

And then, too, there is the prayer. At this moment, Anfield may well lay claim to being the most prayed-for place on earth. Supporters of the Billy Graham Evangelistic Association in over 100 countries have been urged to pray for this summer's meetings. Christians in north-west England have been praying for the friends they brought along in buses, cars and trains tonight. Just as the presence of God seems to hang around those ancient churches where the saints have worshipped down the centuries, a spiritual echo sensed in even a casual visitor's heart, perhaps here, too, the concentrated prayers of thousands – even millions – of people are having some such mysterious effect.

'Where two or three come together in my name, there am I with them.' The Spirit of God is lifting the spirits of men, first into the sheer human enjoyment of being in a good place with good people for a good reason. Later, he will lift them further still. It takes a while for hearts cluttered with the debris which comes from living without God to get attuned to that still, small voice which will sound more clearly than that of the preacher.

Those who view the songs and solos from a safe distance behind a newspaper or in front of a TV set are inclined to dismiss them as part of the process of manipulation; softening up the crowd before pounding them with stark choices. But the armchair philosophers present tonight feel no pressure to conform. Up on the Kop it is positively hard to conform; there are no recognisable gangways and one person working their way towards an exit sends ripples of movement through the crowd and instantly disturbs people's concentration. And while the sound of singing is loud, there is always someone else in view either silently mouthing the words or not opening their lips at all. The uninitiated are present in sufficiently large numbers to be able to take good care of their corporate and individual emotions.

The journalists down on the dusty perimeter track are not concentrating at all. They sense something else in the air; a more than usual evasiveness by the Mission England team has put them on their guard. They are soon rewarded by the unannounced appearance in the directors' box above them of a regal figure wearing a cream suit. Princess Alexandra, and her husband the Hon. Angus Ogilvy, have become the first members of the British Royal Family ever to attend a mission meeting addressed by Billy Graham. Also in the box, and also unannounced but more casually dressed, are famous soccer personalities: Alan Kennedy, Liverpool's star defender; Howard Kendall, manager of nearby rivals Everton; and Bessie Shankly, widow of the Liverpool club's most famous and much loved manager.

But that is tomorrow's news as far as the crowd is concerned; the only special welcome given from the platform by local committee member John Dyer is to the people from the historic city of Chester 30 miles away who have trouped to Anfield in their hundreds tonight. The crowd cheers them as if they were long-lost relatives returned from the ends of the earth, despite the fact that over half those present have already waved their programmes to show they are first time visitors to Anfield.

Meanwhile, there is more music. It is a mixed programme, more traditional than modern, middle-brow; elsewhere there have been muted complaints, mostly from Christians who want more celebration. At least, tonight, everyone can sing along with the easy tunes; visitors can feel comfortable.

The royal guests join in that stirring new song *Majesty* which has become something of a Mission England signature tune this summer. With an orchestral backing tape that seems to leap from a Hollywood epic, it evokes images of triumphal processions, but it looks beyond human regents to the supreme ruler:

> *Majesty, worship His Majesty,*
> *Jesus who died, now glorified, King of all Kings.*

Then there is Wesley's ever popular *O for a thousand tongues*, the last verse a tribute to the musical skills of Cliff Barrows, song leader and compere for most of Billy Graham's meetings over the past 40 years. The 2,000-strong choir and the audience launch in together as one voice without the lead of the piano and organ which accompany most of the hymns. The words are clear enough to be understood by someone who has never heard them before and has no printed programme to follow.

For once, though, American award-winning singer Sandi Patti, back in good shape and voice two months after giving birth to her first child, is upstaged. She hits top C in a shortened version of *Magnify the Lord* but the applause is greater still as Cliff Barrows announces the night's headline-maker; Liverpool Football Club's very own anthem, *You'll never walk alone*.

It is a familiar song in many English soccer grounds. Like the famous *Abide with me* at Wembley Stadium cup final matches, it has a wistful air, a faint if sentimental reminder that life is larger than Saturday's match, and a hymn-like tune which makes it eminently suitable for community singing and which reinforces the view that soccer is, for some, a substitute religion. The Kop has never heard it quite like this, however. It is less raucous – women's voices soften the harsh, mostly male tones of soccer crowds – and there is a word change to suit the occasion. It is all the more powerful for it; this is no baptism of pagan sentiment but a reclamation for Christ of an instinct built into people made in God's image:

> *Walk on, walk on, with CHRIST in your heart,*
> *And you'll never walk alone,*
> *You'll ne-ver walk alone.*

After that we stay with soccer as Joe Brown, youth development officer with Manchester United, stands up to tell the crowd, 'I've found someone who knows tomorrow before I live it.' Gentle country and western singer George Hamilton IV follows, and lets slip that it is his birthday. He is thrown off guard as the choir spontaneously launches into 'Happy birthday, dear George' ('that'll be something I'll tell the grandchildren about'), and after that there is no holding back the audience participation. The sound engineers turn up the loudspeaker volume so that George Hamilton's voice singing *One day at a time* is heard above the uninvited backing group of 32,000. But that is Liverpool, the rearing ground of the Beatles and many other British musicians and comedians.

Its people, with both Welsh and Irish blood, love to sing, and they welcome with open-hearted fun anyone they respect.

The offertory provides a brief lull, an excuse to wriggle and shuffle, to relax and stretch. From the platform comes the usual appeal *not* to put anything in the white plastic buckets as they pass along the rows. 'If you are a visitor or you've been brought by a friend, we do not want you to feel under any obligation to give.' There is a reminder, too, 'that neither Billy Graham nor any of his team receive any remuneration from Mission England. They have come here entirely at their own expense.'

The rumour that American evangelists are in it for the money has never been totally squashed, perhaps because on occasions it is sadly true. The Graham team is sensitive to the issue, but experience has taught them that many Christians who come to the meetings want to give financially at the time; their tickets, after all, have been free and many have come on buses subsidised by local churches.

Wisely, in view of tonight's vociferous audience, Cliff Barrows asks them not to join in Bev Shea's rendering of *Amazing Grace* until the last verse, when the key will change. The veteran singer, now 75, still has a powerful, deep voice, but his arrangements and phrasing reflect his concern to convey a message through his songs; he speaks musically.

> *'Tis grace hath brought me safe thus far*
> *And grace will lead me home.*

The floodlights are on now, growing brighter, it seems as the evening draws in. The brilliant white light pours from the huge pylons in each corner of the stadium, making the darkening sky seem as if great holes have been punched in it to let some unearthly glory, purer, more penetrating than the sun, shine through.

Then, unannounced and without applause, Billy Graham steps to the microphone from his seat in the front row of the platform. It is 8.38 pm; he is beginning later than usual because of the longer preliminaries.

'I asked my wife if she had any suggestions for the message tonight. She said, "Keep it short!"'

Laughter rolls around the stadium, perhaps with a hint of relief in it; the speaker is human and winsome, powerful but not harsh. He does keep it relatively short, too. And for 40 minutes the stadium is as still and quiet as a crowd this size can be.

Up in the seating areas, there are rustles and coughs, fidgetting from stiffness rather than boredom; occasional bustles of activity as the St John Ambulance teams tend to people taken ill. The Kop, with its thousands squatting on cushions, is like the sea on a calm day; never completely silent or motionless, but murmuring rather than roaring, rippling rather than heaving. The authority of the speaker is natural, not forced; he commands attention without demanding it.

Billy Graham preaches on the need to be born again. His voice is crystal clear; he rarely stumbles over, or fumbles for, his words. His message is simple, the same point is made in several different ways, punctuated by anecdotes and true stories. He tells of the Polish Catholic priest he met, who had given himself to Christ after a black woman on a bus in Chicago asked him if he had been born again. There was the Portuguese Surgeon General who found a gospel tract stuck to his shoe. He read it, decided to buy and read a Bible and as a result became a Christian and, later, a Bible teacher.

He gets to the core of his message. 'Billy Graham is a sinner. You're a sinner, and sin is very serious in the sight of God. Its penalty is spiritual death. You can be physically alive but your soul is dead. You'll never find what you are looking for in life until you come to Christ and are born again.'

He tells how he bought a diamond ring on the cheap for his wife. When he had it valued, it turned out to be worth less than he paid for it – it was flawed. So too is the human heart.

'We're born with a tendancy to sin, then we choose to sin, then we become sinners by practice, and we get harder and harder. You may never have another hour like this as long as you live. A radical change is needed in every person for them to be acceptable to the Lord.

'Christ gives a new power to love, to resist the temptations in life. God says, "I'll forgive you, I'll give you eternal life." You can start all over again even if you're 70 years old or even 100 years old. He'll forgive every sin you've ever committed. He'll give you eternal life.'

It is no criticism of Billy Graham to say that his message is unremarkable; there are many preachers able to string words together in cleverer, more colourful ways. Indeed, it is his very ordinariness which has puzzled media and other observers all summer. As the pre-mission advertising leaflet said, 'he uses no gimmicks, no sales talk.'

And yet, when he gets to his famous invitation to make a public act of commitment to Christ – 'I want you to get up out of your seats' – literally thousands of people do. The answer must lie in the biblical concept of spiritual gifts. Billy Graham has the gift of an evangelist; he is someone through whom the Spirit of God works to nudge people off the fence and into the kingdom of heaven. It is not so much what he says which convinces people; it is not even how he says it which persuades them. There is another Power at work as he speaks, which convicts them of sin, of righteousness, and of judgment.

'Why do I ask you to come publicly? I ask you to come publicly because almost everyone who Jesus called in the New Testament he called publicly. Jesus said, "He who acknowledges me before men, I will acknowledge before my father in heaven." Jesus suffered publicly for you; is it too much for you to come publicly to him?'

They come slowly at first, like a dribble from a leaking tap, bobbing over the temporary steps which bridge the perimeter walls normally intended to keep people off the field. Old, young; black, white; male, female: from all quarters of the stadium the dribbles become streams and then rivers converging into a flood in the centre of the pitch, swirling around the platform which rides high above them.

Like drops in the ocean, individuals are hard to distinguish in the crowd, but as they walk forward the harsh floodlights throw them into relief, momentarily emphasising their solitary, public action.

The only sound is like that of rain on a roof: the clatter of tip-up seats and the patter of feet on the stairways. There is no music; no *Just as I am, without one plea* from the choir. The British are too sensitive to the charge of emotional manipulation at this intensely personal, life-changing moment. There is a biblical precedent for pouring cold water, rather than oil, on a sacrifice before praying for fire. There can then be no doubt about the result.

It is an awesome silence; time almost seems to stand still. It slowly lapses into a mild murmur as those first to the front, and those left in the stands, begin to talk quietly as the minutes tick by. Billy Graham calls for quietness, reverence and prayer.

'People are still coming. The night I came they sang two hymns while they waited, and I came on the last verse of the second hymn. I'm glad they waited. You can still come.'

It takes ten, maybe fifteen minutes for everyone to come, and another ten for the evangelist to encourage and exhort them. He reminds them to pray, to read their Bibles, to join a church, and to tell other people they have given their lives to Christ. Then he leads them in a prayer of commitment.

'O God, I am a sinner. I am sorry for my sins. I'm willing to turn from them. I receive Christ as Saviour, I confess him as Lord. From this moment on I want to follow and serve him in the fellowship of his church. Amen.'

Down there on the pitch, open to the sky, the prayers do not hover above people's heads as the songs and assertions had hung briefly around the iron rafters of the stands. Instead, they are muffled and, as it were, whipped away into the air as soon as they are uttered; a transaction with heaven of which the evesdropping multitude heard only the faintest of hints.

The crowd of enquirers – over 3,000 of them – breaks into small groups after the closing prayer. Counsellors pair off with them, talk, pray – often with arms round their shoulders – and note down their names and addresses so they can be linked with 'nurture groups' near their homes. Enquirers are given a pack of literature – a Luke's gospel, a booklet about the Christian life, a card to record their commitment. The choir sings a brief benediction, and all round the stadium people stretch at last, then set off in search of buses parked nose to tail, it seems, for miles around. It is 9.45, almost two hours since we began.

Across the road in Stanley Park, an overflow crowd of maybe a thousand or two has been following the meeting on a huge Diamond Vision screen. All is dark there now, but the sky above is streaked with colour. The floodlights cast a silver halo over the stadium, which fades into a deep heavy turquoise smothering north Liverpool. Out to the west, where the sea is, a thin slice of salmon pink sunset strolls along the horizon.

Many people have met with the Light of the world tonight, and are now on their way back, fearful, perhaps, or exhilerated, into a darker world from which God is often excluded. They have been warned that life will not always be easy; they have been reminded, too, that the hope and joy which is in Christ will never leave their horizon, unlike tonight's sunset.

Somewhere among the throng that still pours steadily from the stadium is a slightly built man with receding hair. Having sat behind the royal guests, he slips away to the car park unrecognised by most of the people he rubs shoulders with.

Like many others on the Mission England team, he will not be in bed before 1.00 a.m. After winding down over a late meal at the team hotel, he will narrate a news report to be phoned through to America for use by many Christian radio stations. There will be papers to sheaf through, decisions to be made, issues to be discussed. His is not the most glamorous of jobs. But nine years ago, in 1975, he began to dream that Billy Graham would lead a major national mission in England. And it was largely through his dogged determination that the dream became a reality...

3

The birth of a vision

Gavin Reid, born 50 years ago north of the Scottish border but now living south of the River Thames, in Surrey, with his wife and three children, has always been a visionary. He first dreamed of another major Billy Graham mission in Britain in 1975, and wrote of his vision in the *Church of England Newspaper*, but that was itself the product of an earlier, and deeper, passion.

A Church of England Minister, the major concern of his life has always been the effective communication of the gospel to people for whom Christian concepts are a foreign language. Because of that, he has sometimes been ahead of his time, an uncomfortable fate shared by pioneers and prophets. While others remain unconvinced of the message they reject the messenger; when they eventually accept it they forget him.

In 1969, while he was the Publications Secretary for the Church Pastoral-Aid Society (CPAS), a support body for evangelicals within the Church of England, he wrote *The Gagging of God*. It exposed the failure of Christians to get out of their religious ghetto and to start living and communicating the Christian faith in ways with which the man in the street could identify.

'To many churches,' he wrote, '"outreach" means opening the church doors wider than usual and waiting for someone to come.... To assume that non-attendance at church-controlled activities is evidence of Godlessness and "hardness of heart" shows a complete lack of understanding of and sympathy with the non-churchgoer.'

He dubbed such an approach to evangelism 'in-drag' – and added that Billy Graham crusades are themselves often 'massive experiments in "in-drag".'

'This is not necessarily a damning criticism of such crusades,' he added. 'The weakness in the large crusade, however, is that there is very little actual breaking of new ground.... If there is to be a genuine outreach in the kind of society structures that we find in modern industrial countries, then Christians will have to be prepared to go it alone into a multitude of circumstances that are not immediately favourable to what they have to say.' Join sports and social clubs, he advocated; use homes instead of halls for evangelistic meetings.

He was not alone in voicing such concerns; the tide of evangelical opinion was already turning. A conference at Keele University in 1967 urged, among other things, that evangelicals should become more culturally aware and socially involved. In a tiny village in the Swiss mountains, American born Francis Schaeffer had begun his 20 years of prodigious literary output, helping many church leaders to relate undiluted biblical faith to a perceptive analysis of contemporary social, cultural and theological uncertainties.

Sometimes in danger, despite his theological orthodoxy, of being labelled as an angry young rebel who older brethren feared would throw the doctrinal baby out with the bathwater of church tradition, Gavin Reid quietly put his beliefs to the test. He was, and is, an evangelist in his own right. In the 1970s he became Secretary of Evangelism for CPAS (now known as Mission at Home). The job enabled him to wrestle with the task of expressing the faith in ways non-Christians could readily identify with, and it also gave him the opportunity to encourage and teach church members to reach out more effectively into their local communities.

It was to be an important training ground; when – much to

his own surprise – he became National Director of Mission England in 1982, he brought to the job practical lessons learned over many years. He thus helped to create a unique project which may well become standard practice in evangelism for years to come, emphasising the training of Christians so that the mission meetings are a huge united exercise in personal evangelism.

Despite his concern for local church and personal outreach, Gavin Reid was also convinced that a major national thrust, providing a focus and stimulus for local initiatives, was necessary. In another book, *The Elaborate Funeral*, he had attempted his own analysis of contemporary British culture. He especially bemoaned the prevailing passive, sponge-like mentality. It soaked up pre-packed information and ideas, and had no means of discerning its truth; the ad-man had become high priest of a consumer society.

The god which failed

Western civilisation in the 1970s was digging its own grave in the mistaken belief that it was digging for gold. The optimism of the 1950s had given way to anxiety in the 1960s. Materialism was a god which had failed to produce the goods, and the shadow of the atomic bomb grew larger and more menacing. There was only one way to go for people whose two-dimensional world had no room for eternal and spiritual perspectives: inwards. The last bastion of freedom was the private realm of home and hearth, which the world outside could pass in a succession of fleeting images on a silver screen and be turned off at will. But self-interest had its uglier side; crime, violence, family breakdown and industrial confrontation grew like fungus on a decaying tree stump.

Christians perceived in differing ways this social and spiritual decline, and the consequent need for evangelism. But to make any powerful impact, rather than merely to scratch the surface, the evangelism had to be concerted, united and large scale. Anything else would be about as effective as sticking pins in the hide of a sleeping elephant.

That meant working together across all kinds of divisions, and that would not be easy.

British Christianity was already well diversified. Quite apart from the denominational divisions, making co-operation difficult at every level, evangelicals – those who accepted Scripture as God's final word in all matters of faith and conduct, and who emphasised the necessity of a personal relationship with the living Christ – were also fragmented and they no longer presented a cohesive cross-denominational force.

For example, there was a growing rift between those who believed they should remain in the established but theologically mixed churches, and those who advocated forming new evangelical fellowships. In 1966 Dr Martyn Lloyd Jones, the minister of Westminster Chapel in London, publicly called for evangelicals to secede from their churches and form an evangelical fellowship.

In the decade which followed another movement, often with a charismatic emphasis, siphoned Christians from the denominations into the so-called house churches. It was not always simply a difference of opinion on church order; it sometimes degenerated into heated slanging matches on the biblical virtues of one or other view.

Furthermore there was a growing concern for mission to be seen as something much more than plucking brands from the fire. It was evidenced by the establishment of agencies such as Tear Fund, providing social and physical help through Christian agencies overseas, and the Shaftesbury Project, stimulating Christian research on contemporary issues.

There was also a growing belief that the day of the large meeting was over, that small groups were the appropriate setting for evangelism in a society reluctant to be told what to do or believe. And the growing confidence and numerical strength of evangelicals within the churches led some of them to focus their attention on their own full programmes of activities, and on denominational affairs. They no longer felt the need for the large co-ordinated activities which in the

past had been so necessary for the encouragement of struggling churches; the social withdrawal into the private,
personal world had its spiritual counterpart.

Any unity in that diversity would be a miracle. But there
was one man who had proved before that under God it could
be achieved: Billy Graham. No one else had the stature to
generate the widespread confidence, trust and co-operation
which characterised that evangelist's ministry around the
world.

Gavin Reid was convinced Billy Graham should be the
focus of a renewed evangelistic foray into Britain. One day,
in 1975, he was asked to attend a meeting which in all
liklihood would issue an invitation to the evangelist to conduct a mission. To many, it seemed a golden opportunity.
But Gavin Reid knew that all that glitters is not gold. He
decided not to go.

Last chance

That meeting, held in Church House, Westminster, in
November 1975, had been prompted by an unexpected phone
call from the manager of Earls Court, a huge exhibition
complex in west London, to Maurice Rowlandson, Director
of the Billy Graham Evangelistic Association (BGEA) in
Britain.

Earls Court had been the scene of Billy Graham's last
major mission in Britain. In June 1966, 18,000 people had
packed the main auditorium, with another 8,000 in adjacent
halls, every night for a month. The following year he returned
for a week's 'All Britain TV crusade', again based on Earls
Court but this time relayed by closed circuit TV to another
26 centres, from Aberdeen in Scotland to Plymouth in Devon.

Due to extensive plans for modernisation and development, Earls Court would never be available again for such
large meetings beyond the end of 1977.

'Have you any plans for another crusade before then?' the
manager asked Maurice Rowlandson. Spurred into action
by the potential deadline, Mr Rowlandson suggested to Lord

Luke, a Christian landowner in Bedfordshire and a long-standing supporter of Billy Graham's work, that he should convene and chair an exploratory meeting.

'I didn't go to that meeting,' Gavin Reid recalls, 'because somehow it didn't seem right to do evangelism just because the hall happened to be free for the last time. Besides, I was already convinced that London was not the right place. I could have said this at the meeting, but I honestly didn't want to appear to oppose Billy Graham.'

In the event, the meeting was inconclusive. Although a large majority of the 109 people present were in favour of an invitation being issued at once to Billy Graham, others were not so sure. They urged further, wider consultations. Already, wide differences of opinion over the wisdom of a Graham crusade, and its nature if it ever happened, were rising rapidly to the surface.

A committee was appointed to work out how such consultations could be taken. A long process of debate, to be studded with bright ideas and abortive initiatives, had begun. It would not be finally concluded for seven years, the time it took for Gavin Reid's middle child to pass through his secondary education and gain a place at university.

Growing concern

The next significant stage was reached in eleven months, however. The committee had suggested that a consultative council should be formed by the Church of England Evangelical Council, the Evangelical Alliance, and the BGEA. This larger group commissioned a working party to produce a report, *Let my people grow*, which was presented in October 1976. Bearing the clear stamp of the forward thinking of Tom Houston, Executive Director of the Bible Society and Chairman of the working party, the report was an ambitious programme for church growth. It envisaged the possibility of a mission led by Billy Graham as part of it. One member of the group was Gavin Reid.

'I was the biggest advocate of Billy Graham,' he now

recalls. 'The others saw the campaign as only one element among many. But I believed that he was essential to make anything happen at all.'

The meeting at which the report was presented revealed the wide diversity of evangelical opinion about the most appropriate way forward for evangelism. The report had a cool reception, and ended up, like so many others, on the shelf.

Meanwhile, there were some new scenes being enacted on the wider church stage which significantly affected the possibility of a Billy Graham mission. The Archbishops of Canterbury and York had already issued a 'Call to the Nation', a bold public attempt to alert the British to their rapidly disintegrating Christian foundations. Archbishop Donald Coggan then announced in April 1977 that the National Initiative in Evangelism (NIE) was to be created. (The name was later changed to *Nationwide* to emphasise its local, rather than large scale, intentions.)

Evangelicals did not have a monopoly of concern for evangelism. Many Christians from different theological perspectives shared the view that the church must evangelise or die. Precisely how to evangelise was something they were equally unclear about, and the NIE, backed by all the main denominations, was intended to supply ideas and inspiration.

It achieved that aim to some extent at a local level, but it failed to stimulate any large scale evangelistic activity. It gradually became clear that here, too, opinion was divided over Billy Graham and that the NIE was not the body to issue an invitation.

Although many evangelicals – including Gavin Reid, by now having won acceptance both as an evangelist and as a church strategist – worked with the NIE, it was clearly too broad to gain the confidence of the whole evangelical constituency. The Evangelical Alliance formed a co-ordinating committee for evangelism in October 1977. Gavin Reid was one of 21 people invited to join it; so too was Clive Calver, then Director of British Youth for Christ.

Time passes quickly on the printed page, but slowly in real

life when you are anxious for action. A year later, in November 1978, Gavin Reid's frustration with the way things were going boiled over. In an article in the *Church of England Newspaper* he wrote of his 'dismay' at the inconclusive results 'of three years of ecclesiastical chatter'. The arguments and consultations had led nowhere. He urged that positive action be taken to invite Billy Graham before the initiative for concerted outreach was lost for ever.

Once more he spelled out his vision. He envisaged Billy Graham visiting several provincial cities rather than London, and that his visit would be preceded by careful training and preparation, and followed by further evangelism. The seed idea of Mission England had been sown again, and this time it did not fall on stony ground.

In March the following year, the BBC Radio 4 religious news programme *Sunday* asked its readers to write in saying whether or not they supported a Billy Graham mission in Britain. Out of a huge mailbag of 14,990 postcards, 13, 925 said 'YES'.

Immediately the momentum began to build up. A private approach was made to Billy Graham by the Evangelical Alliance. A Birmingham schoolmaster, Ken Barnes, convened a meeting of those who 'had lost patience with the consultative procedures currently in progress', to discover the strength of feeling for a Graham mission. In their own attempt to assess the mood, BGEA staff members Walter Smyth and Blair Carlson went to the NIE Assembly at Nottingham to talk to individual delegates; they found much less enthusiasm than the *Sunday* programme, and came away with the message, 'perhaps, but not yet.'

This was significant; the widest impact is based on the widest support, a truth which Mission England was later to prove conclusively. If church leaders on or beyond the fringe of evangelicalism, yet sympathetic to the aims of a Graham mission, were not offering support, then the number of churches working, praying and sending people along would be considerably reduced, and so would the number of people eventually reached with the gospel. Meanwhile, the

Evangelical Alliance had been collecting names of those willing to be associated with a mission.

Developing plans

In January 1980, Billy Graham visited Britain. Three years earlier he had accepted the invitation to speak at two week-long missions at the universities at Oxford and Cambridge in 1980. The attendance almost reached 22,000, and there were over 1800 enquirers; the evangelist had clearly not lost his appeal to the British – nor to their youth. It was an encouraging sign for those who were keen that he should lead a full scale mission.

On 24 March, Billy Graham was in England again, this time to meet a large committee brought together by the Evangelical Alliance. It gave him a formal invitation to lead a mission in 1983 or 1984. A formal answer was expected within a month. It did not come; Billy Graham was uncertain.

At his request a Steering Committee was set up to sift the advice and present a coherent plan for the mission. Business-man David Rennie chaired that meeting of 12 men at London Bible College in May. Gavin Reid had been invited but was unable to attend, so he sent a detailed paper outlining his proposals. After sharing their ideas and reaching a measure of agreement, the others opened his paper; it contained proposals almost identical to theirs.

Also at the meeting were Clive Calver and Eddie Gibbs, who were to play a leading role in the story as it developed further. Eddie Gibbs, also an Anglican minister, was a close friend of Gavin Reid; they had been at theological college together and over the years had often met to talk and to dream together. Now pioneering a church growth depart-ment at the Bible Society, Eddie Gibbs shared his friend's belief that the time was right for a national mission spear-headed by Billy Graham.

They, and the other ten, agreed that a multi-venue mission spread over several months would be the best way forward. But again the evangelist did not feel it was right. He took an agonising five months before he was sure enough to give his answer, although he did not close the door to future approaches.

By now, Gavin Reid had the bit between his teeth. When Billy Graham was passing through London in January 1981, he, Clive Calver and others pressed the evangelist hard, stressing their belief that he was the man to spearhead a new evangelistic thrust. Billy Graham encouraged them to reconvene the Steering Committee and look again at their plans.

This time, Gavin Reid suggested a change of strategy. Instead of getting everyone agreed before inviting Billy Graham, why not get him to say he will come *if* the churches want him, and then go to the country for a response? And instead of sending letters around the world, why not talk the plan out with him face to face? (Legend has it, although Gavin Reid is unable to recall the fact, that the success of Terry Waite, the Archbishop of Canterbury's envoy who had recently secured the release of several British hostages in Iran, inspired the idea. Whether or not it did, it led to Gavin Reid, Eddie Gibbs and Clive Calver being called 'envoys' in all subsequent narrations of the tale.)

And so, on 6 July 1981, the three envoys, with David Rennie and Maurice Rowlandson representing the British BGEA, flew to Nice in the South of France to meet Billy Graham and personally invite him to Britain. They took a revised version of their original multi-mission plan, laying greater stress on the before and after aspects of the three year strategy.

In three hours, they had the answer they had hoped and prayed for. And three years later, to the very day, at Villa Park Birmingham, the three sat together on the platform and watched as the largest number of enquirers – some 5000 – at any of the 1984 meetings came forward; it was one of those delightful coincidences which littered Mission England, and it gave the envoys that extra assurance that their efforts were part of the incomprehensible plans of God.

But in 1981 they had other things on their minds. The offer

of two or three of Billy Graham's months in the summer of 1984 was there, but did British Christians want them? Five public meetings were held to find out, and they were widely advertised to ensure a representative sample of people attended them. They took place during October in Newcastle-upon-Tyne (for the North East), Preston (North West), Coventry (Midlands), Bristol (South West) and Norwich (East Anglia).

London was automatically excluded, not only because Gavin Reid, and Billy Graham, felt that it was time for the evangelist to go to the provinces he had not visited for several decades, but also because Luis Palau had agreed to take a series of missions in the London area in 1983 (and which later extended into 1984). There was no sense in overlapping similar activities.

The envoys, together with Blair Carlson and Walter Smyth of the BGEA, went to each meeting and explained their plan. Mission England would not be just another Billy Graham mission. There would be a whole year of preparation, in which local churches assessed their priorities and trained their members in evangelism and caring for new Christians. The second year would use the regional Billy Graham mission as a focus for evangelism at local church level, followed by a third year of more evangelism centred on local churches. Much of the planning and organisation would be devolved to the regions. Doubts about the follow up of enquirers, often a bone of contention in the past, were allayed for many people as John Mallinson, flown in for the purpose from Australia, described a new approach of 'nurture groups' used successfully in his country.

Within a couple of months, each of the five regions sent invitations to Billy Graham, having set up their own committees following the public meetings. The final united invitation was given to him on 3 March 1982, after the Opera House Theatre complex in Blackpool had been packed to overflowing when he preached there for the two previous nights. That response seemed to be God's confirmation that the time was right; it was certainly an encouragement to believe that once more Billy Graham could be used by God to have a major impact in Britain.

The belief that he could had grown over the preceding years. Lord Tonypandy, a well-known political figure in Britain who, as George Thomas, had fulfilled with distinction the unenviable task of Speaker of the House of Commons, had become honorary chairman of Mission England when the original chairman, Tom Houston, had left Britain to take up the post of President of World Vision International. His comment before the missions began was one of great longing and hope.

'Billy Graham's message is greatly needed in our country at this moment,' he said. 'I am grateful for the way in which Billy Graham is willing to give himself so fully. I welcome beyond measure his return for Mission England. God knows we are in need of a mission and I look forward to hearing the voice of Billy Graham ring through our land once again.'

For Gavin Reid, the forthcoming mission posed a personal problem he had not expected. On his desk that month lay an invitation to become vicar of a large northern church. And yet the experience he had gained over the years, and the respect he had won within both the churches and the BGEA, made him the natural choice to lead Mission England on as its National Director. He opted for Mission England. And if the last seven years had been hard going, the next two were at times nailbiting.

'Up to Christmas 1983 there were many days when I would wake up with a feeling of dread. I was always convinced Billy Graham would go down well, but I had nothing to prove that the level of support would be satisfactory to make the mission really effective.'

Three things happened after Christmas which helped to allay such fears. In January, Billy Graham was in England for a brief visit. His most publicised engagement was to preach before the Queen at Sandringham, where he had spent the weekend as her guest. Unusually, for a private visit, the Queen allowed a photocall after the service. The national press published pictures of the evangelist with the Queen, and presented him as a statesman who commanded royal respect.

A few days later, he met, again privately, with the Archbishop of Canterbury and about 50 other British church leaders from all the major denominations at Lambeth Palace. The Archbishop made no secret of his respect for Billy Graham, and the meeting gave the evangelist an opportunity to explain his purpose and aim. The leaders gave him a warm welcome, a fact which no doubt further encouraged 25 or so Anglican bishops who publicly supported Mission England by attending the meetings and encouraging their clergy and people to do the same.

And the strength of grassroots support was shown when over 11,000 clergy and lay leaders from churches all over England went to hear Billy Graham speaking in Birmingham; only about 4,000 had been expected when the meeting was arranged, at relatively short notice, in December.

Mission England had been born. But the small group of midwives who had attended the birth were no longer sufficient to ensure that their special infant would grow to maturity. They could guide its development, but its success or failure would now depend on the work of tens of thousands of people.

At first, however, it needed a few hundred to help it through the kindergarten; people like Ruth Dyer, for example, who lives with her husband and children in a small west country village, and who quickly caught the vision of what Mission England was all about...

4

Preparing the way

Ruth Dyer faced a daunting challenge. The embryonic South West regional committee of Mission England had asked her to be chairman of the women's task group. (The title 'task group' was preferred to 'committee' from the outset because the object was work, not talk.)

Her job was to get Christian women praying, building bridges of friendship with their neighbours and friends, and sharing their faith, all as part of the general thrust of Mission England, and with the Billy Graham visit as a focal point. Her primary area of concern covered five English counties (although the region as a whole was larger still) with major towns often 50 miles or more away from Bristol, the nearest centre hosting Billy Graham meetings.

If she had been in charge of, say, the stadium task group, her job would have been very specific with clear practical objectives which could be seen and measured; build a platform, get seats and cushions, create access to the turf from the stands. Or if she had to organise a large choir it would have been relatively easy to find willing helpers in the main towns, and through them arrange practices for volunteers; lots of Christians like to sing. But getting ordinary church members, their time already occupied with raising families, running homes, going out to work, leading Sunday Schools, to pray for and witness to their non-Christian friends – where was she to start?

She began by practising what she was commissioned to preach; she prayed. Then she sent out a letter about Mission England, in order to enlist prayer support, to every denominational and para-church group she could think of...

Church of England; that's easy. Bristol Diocesan HQ, Bath and Wells Diocesan HQ. And the evangelical group, CPAS Women's Action (Western Region).

Baptist; harder. No overall women's structure. So it's got to be the ministers – in the Bristol, Bath, Wells, Weston-super-Mare, Gloucester, Cheltenham and Taunton associations.

Methodists; they have a Women's fellowship, so write to local secretaries in Gloucester, Cheltenham, Swindon, Marlborough, Yeovil and Weston-super-Mare.

Catholics; straightforward. Catholic women's guild. And the Bishop of Clifton.

Pentecostals; Independent Evangelicals, United Reformed, Brethren.

Salvation Army; write round the Bristol area.

Then there's the para church groups; Women's World Day of Prayer, Lydia Prayer Fellowship, Know Your Bible group leaders, Evelyn Christenson Prayer Chain, Bristol Council of Churches.

After that, there's all the women I know personally in the South West, who would be key people for prayer and outreach.

I think I'll make a pot of tea...

And after that, there was the task group to appoint, people who would represent strategic places and who could discuss ideas, organise activities and spread the word; *Invite task group*. To share ideas and fellowship, the group would need to meet regularly; *arrange regular meetings*. More people would be needed as contacts in each local area; *appoint area representatives*. Being a nebulous task, it needed some *plan of campaign; set up admin procedure*. It sounds a bit armchair bound; people are best enlisted to pray and become involved in Mission England if they meet the chairman face to face; *visit throughout region, encourage area reps, speak at meetings*. That also means more letters, more phone calls, very early mornings and very late nights; *and lots of prayer*. Another cup of tea?

Of course, it would have been quite straightforward if Ruth Dyer had not been ill. She had had problems with a bad throat, high temperature and general weakness for some months; it got worse just after she took over her Mission England role in June 1983. Doctors said it was likely she would have to remain on medication for the rest of her life.

The day before she was due to go to hospital for tests, she was at home watching the Wimbledon tennis tournament on TV. She felt weak and unwell, and longed for someone to come and pray with her. The doorbell rang; it was the minister of a neighbouring church. He did not know Ruth Dyer, but had felt compelled to come to the house and pray for healing and the restraint of evil.

That prayer was powerfully answered, and she was healed and able to continue her Mission England work.

People's mission

Ruth Dyer was one of a hundred or more people doing the same kind of work in their spare time all over England. Each region had its own task groups for prayer, publicity, visitation, choir, stadium, counselling and follow-up, youth and so on. There were area chairmen and task groups, too, attempting to encourage and co-ordinate Mission England interest and activity in smaller localities throughout each region.

It was a vast, and at times loose network, arranged not, as so many committees are, to rubber-stamp the decisions and obey the dictates of some central mafia, but because there was no central mafia. Mission England was conceived as a mission of the people to the people. If Ruth Dyer *et al* had not mobilised, enthused and organised hundreds of others, then there would have been correspondingly less prayer, less outreach, less effectiveness, less joy, and fewer new Christians, before, during and after Billy Graham's brief visit.

There were national guidelines, of course, for some of the roles. Strategy was the responsibility of the national leadership. But tactics were in the hands of the people at the front line.

It could not have been done any other way. England is not a monolithic country with a uniform culture. Regions vary considerably; some are relatively prosperous, others are considerably depressed. Some have strong church life, and others do not; some are dominated by one denomination. The English have never been a single race, because they do not spring from a single stock. Although twentieth century mobility has softened the regional differences, the language and the lifestyle as well as the architecture and the agriculture, are sufficiently varied to take the unsuspecting traveller by surprise. But if any one thing does unite them, it is the dislike of being told what to do by people who live in London (and even more by those who live in Brussels). The British bulldog is its own master.

This was evidenced from the beginning on the national committee. 'In the early meetings we were each boxing in our corners,' Mission England vice-chairman David Rennie recalls. 'It took us some while to build real fellowship.'

The solution which was eventually adopted – to the considerable frustration of some strong spirits – was to form a Federal Board. It would direct overall strategy, but leave the regions to evolve their own tactics so long as they kept within prescribed guidelines. Each region would be represented by Directors on the Board, which was so structured that non-regional directors (that is, the national leaders) could never outnumber (and thus outvote) the regions.

To first earn respect and trust, rather than to impose plans and methods was, it transpired, an effective if at times tedious and even agonising way of ensuring that the unity and co-operation which the venture required was deep and true. Patience, fourth in Paul's list of the Spirit's ninefold fruit, appears to be a direct product of the preceding three: love, joy and peace; it leaves no room for rushing to fulfil a vision by trampling over those adjudged to be in the way.

By early 1983, there were three main strategists. Gavin Reid, seconded from CPAS (Mission at Home), Eddie Gibbs, seconded from the Bible Society, and Brian Mills, seconded from his role in stimulating evangelism through the Evangelical Alliance. Clive Calver had also been seconded from British Youth For Christ, but he had to pull out of Mission England in the spring when he became full-time General Secretary of the Evangelical Alliance.

Each had specific responsibilities. The triumvirate was flat-topped but Gavin Reid, as National Director, assumed overall responsibility, and therefore had close involvement with finance, publicity, management and policy. Eddie Gibbs became Director of Training and Follow-up, developing courses for preparing church members for witness and systems for helping new Christians integrate into the churches. Brian Mills as Assistant Director shouldered a variety of disparate roles – youth, prayer, women's groups, and extension ministry (evangelism outside the stadium meetings but during the mission period in each venue).

A national office was set up at Harrow, a 20-minute rail ride from central London, in premises belonging to an electronics company founded by David Rennie. Each region also established an office to handle local activities and arrangements. In Ipswich it was a slender portable cabin parked in the yard of Ipswich Town Football Club; in Birmingham it was a huge room draped with colourful woollen tapestries in a once-elegant city-centre building.

But these offices were usually small, with only a few full-time staff – and even fewer who were actually paid. Anthony Bush, a farmer near Bristol, used to working a 90 hour week, commuted to the office between morning and afternoon milking, and drew no salary. The National Administrator, Roy Slack, who ran the Harrow office and was responsible as Company Secretary to oversee the business arrangements in each region, took early retirement from the National Health Service to work with Mission England, again drawing no salary, although also working a few hours a week for a local medical committee. Formerly Chief Administrator in the Bexley (Kent) Health Authority, he was not the only highly qualified person to join Mission England at comparatively little or even no cost to it. John Sherman in Ipswich had retired early from a senior position with the oil company BP;

John Williamson in the North West had been General Manager and Director of Royal Insurance, a large Liverpool-based group.

Even the three national leaders were seconded from their own organisations, and thus placed no financial burden on the project. British Christians have always preferred to have their evangelism on the cheap. With Mission England they got it – but for once without sacrificing quality. And they also got their priorities right; rather than build a towering superstructure of administration, they laid a deep foundation of prayer.

Caught by prayer

David Brumpton was a revolutionary socialist. At home in the Midlands, the family often seemed to be at war; his eldest daughter, Karon, was a Christian and took most of her father's verbal barrage as he sought to educate her to his revolutionary ways.

'My wife, Audrey, acted as referee, trying her best to calm the situation,' he recalls. 'Little wonder that Karon broke the news of her baptism with trepidation.

'Surprisingly my reaction was one of intrigue, and I accepted the offer of advice from our Pastor with gratitude. To witness my daughter's joy in baptism was to me a revelation, and several weeks later both my wife and I asked the Lord to come into our lives.

'Shortly afterwards I learned that throughout these uncertain times, we had been in the prayers of a 'triplet group' and the news warmed my heart as I realised the power of prayer and the part it played in making us a family at peace, peace with one another and the peace of knowing the Lord Jesus as our saviour.'

Prayer triplets were the brainchild of Brian Mills; like all really effective and popular ideas, this one was stunningly simple. It was nothing more nor less than three people (or three couples) agreeing to pray regularly *with* each other *for* nine others (three names per person). Three people could be more free and flexible than a larger group to meet informally; they would not feel inhibited for long if they were unused to praying aloud in groups; Jesus had spoken about 'two or three meeting in my name;' it is more encouraging to pray together than alone, and scripture implies it is also more powerful; and nine people to pray for was a challenge but not a marathon.

Some 90,000 prayer triplet cards, on which group members formally wrote down their commitment, were requested from the regional offices during the year before the Billy Graham missions. Brian Mills believes many more groups were meeting than the 30,000 which this implies. But even if there were not, the prayer triplet scheme mobilised regular, specific prayer for over a quarter of a million non-Christians like David Brumpton. And like him, many found Christ long before Billy Graham reached English shores.

One married couple in the North East were placed on a prayer triplet list at the very start of Mission England. They became Christians during 1983, and attended a Mission England training course. Following that, they were accepted to work as counsellors at the stadium meetings in 1984, helping enquirers come to personal faith in Christ.

Also in the North East, a counsellor talked with a young boy who was unable to tell him what church had invited him to the Billy Graham meeting in Sunderland. A girl behind him stepped forward and supplied the details. She said that she and two friends had prayed for the boy on the prayer triplet scheme. All the others had become Christians; he was the last.

'As I was going out of the stadium, I saw this girl with two others kneeling in prayer. They were obviously the prayer triplet, giving thanks to God. The sight of those three girls praying will be the one thing that I will remember about Mission England most of all.'

Prayer triplets happened in all sorts of places. One was reported on a North Sea oil rig. There were a considerable number at the Porton Down chemical research centre in the South West. They were popular in schools and homes.

It was not the only form of prayer encouraged during the Mission England build-up, however. Women's groups often organised neighbourhood prayer groups and larger meetings. Brenda Huddleston, Ruth Dyer's counterpart in East Anglia (North), tells of a praise and prayer meeting which was packed out.

'We couldn't stop the ladies first praising and then praying for four and a half hours. One lady prayed for her mother who had rejected her as a young child. She has since been reunited with her and the daughter, now in her 40s, has been able to forgive her mother.'

Something very new to British Christians was the suggestion of inviting non Christians to neighbourhood prayer meetings. The fears of ridicule and the hackles of biblical separation immediately rise, but American Millie Dienert had been touring the country assuring women's groups that it worked, so some thought they had better try it. Like Sheila, for example.

'After cowardly procrastination for three days I went out and knocked on doors of my immediate neighbours, and was really humbled by the response, for five came and only two of them sometimes attended church.

'On the first evening one of them said, "I'm so glad you invited me for this evening because today is the anniversary of my sister's death, and I feel so bitter about the lack of proper attention she had. It's just what I need – a time of quiet and prayer."'

A scheme which combined prayer and practical faith-sharing was Operation Andrew, no more than a slightly formalised method of friendship evangelism. It was something for individuals; they were encouraged to pray for up to seven others who they would try to invite to hear Billy Graham. There was a card for them to write down the names as a reminder. (The act of writing down a name, trivial as it sounds, often has the effect of sealing a promise to oneself, and turning an intention into a commitment.)

The Billy Graham team knew from their long experience that 80 per cent of people who become Christians at mission meetings have been taken to them by Christian friends. The reason is obvious. They have been prayed for and talked to for some time. They have begun to realise already that Christianity is not so foolish as they once thought, and are prepared to attend a Christian meeting. They have possibly discerned some inner resource their friend has which they admire or desire. In biblical terminology, the seed has been sown and watered; it awaits the harvester.

Operation Andrew takes its name from the New Testament incident when Andrew the fisherman met Jesus. The first thing he did was to fetch his brother to meet Jesus too. And, as Billy Graham was fond of emphasising, the idea was not an American export.

'You taught it to us,' he said. 'We first came across it here in England in 1954 during the Harringay crusade. Now we encourage it all over the world. It's been a means God has used to bring countless people to himself.'

It is not usually the easiest of things to talk to a friend, or a stranger, about spiritual matters. However much preachers harangue congregations to go and tell others about Christ, the fact remains that Christian commitment *is* a personal thing, and for some people the thought of describing it to others is akin to the prospect of undressing in public. But personal as it is, faith in Jesus Christ is not private, because it radically affects the way people speak and act, live and work. It is an inward contract with outward consequences.

For Mission England, it was not enough to *tell* people to pray in threes and talk one to one; it had to be *taught*.

Taught to speak

Sudbury in Suffolk is an attractive East Anglian market town immortalised as 'Eatanswill' in Charles Dickens' *Pickwick Papers*, and noted as the birthplace of the English portrait and landscape painter Thomas Gainsborough. With hardly a snowflake to be seen, 1984 crept meek and mild into its hedgerows; George Orwell's spectre of Big Brother is far less believable among its half-timbered houses than even the

larger-than-life figure of Mr Samuel Pickwick and his friends
Snodgrass, Tupman and Winkle embroiled in election fever
and fisticuffs outside the town hall.

It was one of many places throughout England where in
February and March that year Christians from several local
churches joined together for a series of four *Christian Life and
Witness* classes.

Through the courses, they were reminded of the basic
truths of the Christian message and how to live out the faith
they professed. They were given help in answering common
objections to Christianity, and in leading another person to
know Jesus Christ personally.

From the 49,980 people in England who attended these
classes were drawn the counsellors for the Billy Graham
meetings. Those who volunteered for counselling attended a
fifth training session and had a brief personal interview
before being accepted for the task.

The object of the course was not only to supply manpower
for meetings, but also to equip people for evangelism.
According to the townsfolk of Sudbury, it more than achieved
its objective.

'I wanted to witness. This course has shown me how to do
it.'

'I feel a more earnest desire then I have ever experienced
to win other souls to Christ.'

'My prayer life has got so much better since I started this
course.'

'It has encouraged me to witness – to stand by my faith.
Satisfied a need in me.'

'It has made me love the Lord more deeply. Praise the
Lord!'

During the courses, some 800 people across England said
they had committed their lives to Christ for the first time as a
result of the teaching. Eddie Gibbs suggests that it was the
largest Christian training exercise ever conducted in Britain.

The course had been adapted from the normal Billy
Graham training manual by Eddie Gibbs. To the Americans,
the British insistence on adapting tried and tested material

seemed at first irksome and even arrogant. But the British
bulldog can sniff a cultural invader from a mile off, and while
he wrinkles his nose still further misses the point of the
message it brought. In biblical parlance, stumbling blocks
are to be removed, not erected, for believer and unbeliever
alike. One seemingly minor but in fact major change was to
redesign all the literature and print it in English typefaces;
even the Americans recognised it made an improvement.

More far reaching were the changes to the counselling
material given to enquirers. The BGEA had always used
John's Gospel, and had adopted the New International
Version. The British leadership insisted that Luke's Gospel
in the Good News version was more appropriate at the time
in England. John makes considerable demands on a new
Christian with what for many are unfamiliar and difficult
concepts and word-pictures; Luke gives the facts about Jesus
in a less complicated way. It could no longer be assumed in
Britain, following a decline in Sunday School attendance,
that enquirers knew the facts about Jesus. Babies need to
drink milk before they can be expected to digest meat.

To complete the process, the children's counselling
material was entirely altered, and an innovation (for the
BGEA) introduced: counselling packs for teenagers. (In the
event these only proved suitable for youngsters up to the age
of 14.)

Eddie Gibbs and the Mission England 'concept committee'
worked over their proposed changes with the BGEA until
both groups were happy with the product. It gave the British
a different picture of their allegedly intransigent cousins who
insisted on doing evangelism their way.

'I want to place on record my gratitude to their willingness
to make changes,' Eddie Gibbs said at the conclusion of the
Billy Graham missions. It was a two-way relationship which
he forged with Charlie Riggs and Tom Phillips, BGEA
counselling and follow-up maestros, and the rest of the team.
'They have jolted us and show us how painfully negative we
are. We don't *expect* to achieve anything in evangelism and
church life, so we *don't*.'

Another and vital aspect of mission, follow-up of converts, was given new emphasis by the Mission England leadership, resulting in another training course called *Caring for new Christians*. A frequent criticism of large scale evangelism had been voiced during the seven years' debate over the advisability of another Graham mission; not enough is done to help enquirers stick in the churches, it was said.

In Sydney, Australia, in 1979, the concept of nurture groups had been first established, and it was applied in England on a scale 'which we've never had before,' according to Billy Graham. A nurture group is a six-session Bible study course to help new Christians come to terms with the basic facts and application of their new-found faith. From the beginning it became a Mission England rule: enquirers would only be referred for follow-up to recognised nurture groups.

To be counted as a fully participating church, a local fellowship had to have its own nurture group structure in place before the mission began. Neighbourhood interdenominational groups were established to cover areas on the map where there were no participating churches within easy reach of enquirers. Church ministers would, as a matter of courtesy, be informed of any of their regular members who had gone forward, but responsibility for follow-up was not directly referred to them. The system was called 'dual referral'.

Some 30,000 people went through *Caring for new Christians*, the requirement for any nurture group leader. Churches were asked to nominate a person who had been on the course to whom referrals would be sent. In retrospect one weakness emerged, in that potential nurture group leaders were not interviewed as prospective counsellors were; enthusiasm or concern are not always accompanied by aptitude.

The courses were generally taught by people who had themselves first been trained by Eddie Gibbs and other British and American leaders. At Lindley Lodge in Warwickshire in the autumn of 1983, for example, 100 people were prepared to lead courses, and another 50 were trained later. However, more trainers were required, and again a weakness emerged in that there was not always central control over their selection. One region even left the selection of trainers to local areas, leading to one occasion at least when a trainer was talking through his own counselling experience more than taking his audience through the course exercises.

Two other training courses were also prepared. *Is my church worth joining?* encouraged local churches to take a critical look at their own structures in preparation for receiving an influx of new members. Adapted from a Bible Society course, it was used by some 5,000 people. A study course on personal evangelism, *Care to say something?*, for use by individuals or groups, completed the quartet.

Jack sat through a Billy Graham sermon in Bristol, disappointed with it and feeling certain few people would come forward. He was a trained counsellor.

'However, at the appeal, everything changed. From the training I had expected a steady trickle at first with maybe a few more when they knew they weren't the first to go. In the event I witnessed what I could only describe as water flowing from a mountain side into the bowl of the stadium as if snow had suddenly melted. I knew I had to go with them and the realisation came to me that this was nothing to do with Billy Graham or anyone else – what I was witnessing was a mass answer to many prayers over many months. The whole event took on a new meaning and at that point all the training and emphasis of Mission England fell into place.'

Getting it together

Car journeys are not renowned for their creative potential, but one which Gavin Reid shared with Peter Horrobin, a Methodist and Mission England committee member in the North West, proved the exception. In discussing the music for the mission meetings they conceived the idea of a new hymnbook, *Mission Praise*.

There was no shortage of hymn and chorus books already in print. 'But we went ahead with the book because we saw it would have a real bridge-building role between the different spiritualities,' said Gavin Reid. 'It could prove the ideal supplement to the standard hymn books. We felt this could be a real Mission England ministry.'

Mission Praise was launched in November 1983 with large meetings addressed by Cliff Barrows, BGEA music director, in each of the six regions. Over 11,000 people attended them, and, perhaps more significant, almost 3,000 people signed up to volunteer as choir members, stewards or other helpers at the Billy Graham meetings.

It was not the only series of meetings held as part of the preparation for Mission England. *Prepare the Way* was a music and preaching tour in the spring of 1983 organised by Clive Calver and British Youth for Christ on behalf of Mission England. Attended by some 46,000 people, many of them young, it proved to be a powerful challenge to Christians to get out of their seats and begin serious evangelism in their communities.

A follow-up tour in the Midlands region, *Here is your God*, drew audiences totalling 10,000 in small towns from Ross on Wye in the Welsh border country to Northampton midway between Birmingham and London. Quadraplegic artist Joni Eareckson Tada toured the regions, and at one meeting in Lowestoft, in East Anglia, all 800 tickets were sold and a further 200 people listened to her at an overflow relay in a nearby hall.

Former American astronaut James Irwin, the first person to walk on the moon, told some 10,000 people in East Anglia (South) alone that 'Jesus walking on the earth is more important than man walking on the moon.' And Fiona Castle, wife of British entertainer Roy Castle, also visited that region among others to speak of her faith and how God rescued her marriage and healed her son.

When she went to Newmarket, another minor miracle got her there. She was not on the train which organisers had met, and the next was not due for an hour – well after the meeting was scheduled to begin. One of the organisers felt compelled to return to the station after a few minutes, however – and there was Fiona Castle. Her connecting train at Cambridge had not waited for the one she was on from London. But British Rail took the (almost) unheard-of step of laying on a special train to get her and her fellow passengers to Newmarket.

Ministers' meetings also played an important part in the preparation process, as the concept of Mission England was explained to local church leaders by the national and regional organisers. If ministers were not behind the concept, their members were unlikely to benefit from the training or take part in the outreach. (One exception was reported from the North East, where the elders of a free church refused to support the mission officially because of alleged 'compromise' over Roman Catholic involvement. They in turn compromised by saying that individual members could join in if they wished. To their surprise a large proportion of them did, signing on as counsellors, stewards and choir members, and to their even greater surprise some 90 enquirers were referred to the church's nurture groups.)

One minister in East Anglia went to a meeting having many suspicions. Afterwards he commented, 'This is very, very good. My fears are allayed. I can now back Mission England.'

Perhaps the largest interdenominational leaders meeting the country has ever seen was held in January 1984. Over 11,000 clergy and lay leaders trekked to hear Billy Graham speaking in the snow-covered National Exhibition Centre at Birmingham. 'I come on my knees as your servant,' he declared. Many leaders returned to their churches determined to become fully involved in the missions, even though by then the preparations were already well in hand.

Pasting it up

Public relations work of another kind was also required as the missions drew closer. Personal invitations to friends and neighbours were reinforced by a publicity and visitation campaign.

Publicity gave the national leadership several hurdles to

clear. Two objections soon surfaced; one was the cost, the other the concept. The idea of spending up to £50,000 per region on posters and newspaper advertisements is beyond the experience of most British Christians and even Christian organisations. Some regional committee members thought it was bad stewardship, especially when the BGEA said that only a small percentage of people came into meetings solely through having seen the publicity.

Budgets were at times revised downwards, until at the eleventh hour the need was realised and costings were assessed more realistically. Regions constantly under-estimated their requirements for leaflets and posters, causing shortages of supply and last minute reprints.

The simple posters, designed by the Christian Principal of a professional agency, featured a smiling Billy Graham printed in black over a soft red background of London's Wembley Stadium where he had preached on the closing day in the 1966 mission. Apart from details of the local meetings, the only words were: *Billy Graham – worth listening to.*

Objections came from several quarters. Some wanted a harder sell: 'Come and hear him!' Others wanted it to be more colourful and sophisticated; the proposals were old-fashioned looking, they said. And still others wanted a stronger Christian content, with God or a biblical text mentioned in the wording.

But at this point the national leadership, supported by the advisory publicity committee, was adamant. The committee had tried to think through the campaign from first principles.

'Many Christians simply do not know how to speak to the world in terms it understands,' was Gavin Reid's constant complaint. 'People are hungry for the gospel, but they tend to reject the religiosity which they rightly or wrongly associate with God words on posters.'

The aim of the publicity was to create an awareness of the event so that Christians could offer, and non-Christians accept, invitations to the meetings without feeling embarrassed or pressured. The missions became public property through the publicity, and sparked off conversations which could be turned easily to the purpose of the missions.

To the charge that the publicity emphasised a man more than a man should be emphasised in Christian work, the committee answered that the world at large is interested in people more than ideas; people respond to people, and if they like them they will take what they say seriously. Billy Graham often said that he had had to reluctantly accept the fact; he would much prefer his name did not appear at all, but he recognised that it brought people to the meetings.

The posters were to be simple and in two colours partly because they were cheaper, and partly because the publicity committee did not want to do anything which would foster the impression that the meetings were exercises in slick salesmanship by money-laden Americans; the spectre of Elmer Gantry still haunts the collective unconscious.

There was to be no reference to God or a biblical text because the sole purpose of the publicity was to create an awareness of the meetings and not to preach the gospel. The gospel would be made very clear at the meetings, but it would be of little value if people did not go through the turnstiles. Although the committee spent some time trying to accommodate the concern felt by others, they could find no form of words which did not at once run the danger of awakening some stereotype or preconceived idea in non-Christian minds and thus putting them off the message before they had even heard the messenger.

Billy Graham once said that all the effort of the meetings would be worthwhile even if only one person became a Christian. Perhaps the same could be said of the publicity. Mary, a student from Ireland, had not intended to go to the meetings. But one day while out shopping, everywhere she turned she saw a poster about the mission.

So she said, 'All right, Lord, I'll go and hear Billy Graham.' She joined the crowds at Roker Park, Sunderland, and went forward to give her life to Christ. She said it was the best night she had ever had, and she was going to phone her grandmother in Ireland at 10.30 pm, knowing how pleased she would be at the news.

In the three weeks before each mission, homes were visited throughout the region. Visitors had a leaflet for each home, but they were under strict instructions not to put it through the letterbox but to knock and hand it over personally. They were to give a friendly invitation to the meetings. Each leaflet was overprinted with details of where transport was arranged from the locality.

Some three to four million homes in England were contacted during that time. The visits resulted in some people coming to the meetings who had no other church contact. Midlands region visitation task group chairman Alan Betteridge calculated that one or two people came to the meetings for every 100 homes visited; not a high return on the time invested, but in fact amounting to between 1,000 and 2,000 people in Birmingham's Villa Park stadium every night who would not have otherwise come under the sound of the gospel.

It helped the large meeting to become relevant to the local street; it brought the personal touch to what might have seemed an impersonal event. It had its moments. One lady was rebuffed by a man who refused the literature, said he was an atheist and that he would go to hell. When she had visited the street and was walking back, she saw the man being carried out of his house on a stretcher and put in an ambulance.

Another visitor was also rebuffed, this time by a woman. The visitor was also a counsellor, and after the first meeting of a mission she was on the grass in the counselling area and approached a woman to talk to her. The woman said, 'You don't know me but I know you. I refused to take your literature from you when you came to my door.' She had none the less gone to the meeting and at the invitation had walked forward to give her life to Christ.

And that happened on 12 May 1984, in Bristol, in South West England. After a year of preparation by local churches, the Billy Graham phase of Mission England was about to begin...

5

Shipshape and Bristol fashion

Ashton Gate, Bristol, 12–19 May

On Saturday 12 May 1984, in Bristol, Billy Graham addressed his first large-scale meeting in England for 17 years. If the audience followed the normal pattern for Graham meetings, then over a third of those present would have been no more than toddlers when he was speaking to the nation from Earls Court in 1967. Would they respond as a previous generation had?

Furthermore, it was the first series of multi-site missions ever conducted on this scale in England. Each mission was relatively short; there was little time for a build-up of local public interest. Consequently, no-one knew what to expect; there were only hunches and hopes. But Mission England's South West Regional Director, Anthony Bush, was confident.

'I feel assured that God is going to do something that is going to be, in his terms, extremely special and important,' he told Margaret Collingwood of the *Church of England Newspaper* in an interview published the day before. 'I don't know if it will be numerically or in depth.'

There were two factors which gave him and his committee some grounds for their optimism. One was the high advance bookings. Over 500 buses had reserved parking space for the first night, and some 33,000 free tickets had been distributed. But would the buses be full? And how many of the tickets would become warm bodies on stadium seats? BGEA experience warned that actual attendance could frequently be a third less than the advance bookings.

The second factor was a remarkable Gallup Poll which caused Gordon Heald, Managing Director of the Gallup Organisation in Britain, to send his researchers back to double-check their results. It indicated that 93 per cent of people in Bristol had heard about the mission. One third said they were likely to go to Ashton Gate, and almost two thirds believed that Billy Graham had something relevant to say to people in Britain today.

Although open to criticism, in that the interviews were conducted only with people who had been to church at least once in the previous year (which is said to account for nearly half the total population), the Poll revealed a far higher degree of awareness than that normally achieved by commercial companies with much larger marketing budgets than Mission England. Religion and Billy Graham were out in the market place.

Such indeed was their confidence that the committee agreed at a late stage to add £30,000 to their budget by hiring the huge Diamond Vision TV relay screen. Some 30 feet wide, this Japanese innovation is made up of tiny TV screens in a matrix which provides a brilliant picture in broad daylight. Mounted on the black trailer of an articulated truck it was placed in Ashton Gate Park, separated from the stadium by a single row of nineteenth century terraced houses. It was the only one of its kind in Britain at the time.

Saturday 12 May dawned fair. The sun shone, but a brisk breeze sent the cotton-wool clouds skidding across the sky, and kept the air feeling cool. It also roared down Billy Graham's clip-on microphone, occasionally sending a sound like that of snorting horses across the stadium.

By 2.30 p.m., an hour before the meeting was due to start, Ashton Gate was slowly filling up. Some 7,500 extra chairs had been spread like a fan round three sides of the playing area, the second largest in all four divisions of the English Football League. They were open to the elements, but close to the central platform, and this had the important effect of drawing crowd and speaker nearer to each other, and of creating a relaxed atmosphere. People inevitably sat on the grass as well as on the chairs, and it soon became more like a summer's outing than a religious service.

The choir behind the platform was clad in red and blue plastic caghouls bought by the local committee to protect the singers against the cold and rain (the roof of the stand did not project over their seats). As they began warming up around ten minutes to three, there were still large gaps in the terraces at each end of the stadium, but the seats were filling up fast.

And when Cliff Barrows stepped to the microphone at 3.30 p.m., Ashton Gate *felt* full. There was still plenty of room on the terraces, but 31,000 people had turned up; the confidence had been justified.

Some of those thousands had travelled a long way. Bristol is served by motorways running north, east and west, but residents in the region would normally relate to the larger towns nearer their homes rather than to Bristol. However, 58 buses came from the county of Cornwall, well over 100 miles away, and 30 from Plymouth and the Torbay area almost as far distant. Sixty four had crossed the sleek Severn Bridge from south Wales. A special train from Exeter, the region's second largest city, had been fully booked for some weeks; three other charter trains came from elsewhere in the region. The local Bristol bus company hired out all its spare vehicles to church groups. In all, 570 buses and 6,000 cars drove in. Any fears that the first day's attendance was artificially high just because it was the first day were soon allayed. For the next five days between 25,000 and 31,000 people came to each meeting; on the final two days the attendance soared to 36,500 and 38,000 – the latter only 4,000 short of Bristol City Football Club's ground record for a soccer match.

Ashton Gate seemed to have elastic sides and while some people had to stand on the terraces for the final two meetings, there was not the uncomfortable squash that was to occur in other places later in the summer. The Diamond Vision screen was not needed, although groups of people stopped in the park to watch it who would never have entered the stadium.

So the crowds came; getting them there on time, however, gave one man quite a headache.

Bridge building

Roger Lilley had a problem: he needed parking space for 500 buses in an area of closely-packed houses and factories. End to end the buses would have stretched for about four miles. And they would all converge on the stadium during a single hour.

So he took two weeks off from his job in insurance, and visited all the factories around Bristol's Ashton Gate football ground. Several of them offered their yards and other open space, and he then devised routes from all directions into the complex one-way system round the ground. When the crowds poured in to hear Billy Graham, no-one had to walk more than a quarter of a mile from bus to stadium.

Unfortunately, most of them had to cross Winterstoke Road, a busy dual carriageway feeding the main road out of Bristol to the south west. Up to 15,000 pedestrians surging across any road is a recipe for traffic chaos – and personal injury. The answer would be a bridge, assuring steady, if slow, progress across the road with minimal traffic disruption.

Regional director Anthony Bush made 55 telephone calls before he eventually got it a week before the mission was due to begin. Getting the materials was relatively easy; getting someone to erect the bridge was the problem. Eventually, a Christian in the army gave him the contact he needed – and the 100th Field Regiment of the Territorial Army (Britain's volunteer reservists) built a scaffold footbridge during a public holiday the weekend before the mission, glad of the experience it gave them.

It was not the only transportation triumph. To keep as much traffic out of the stadium area as possible, the organisers persuaded British Rail to re-open a railway station near Ashton Gate; it had been closed for 20 years as a result of economies made in the 1960s. A rail shuttle service ran round the city, giving many of its half-million inhabitants the opportunity of a cheap and easy ride to hear Billy Graham.

Not everyone found the travelling easy, however. On the Sunday, one couple, well-known leading figures in the community, drove round for an hour trying to find a parking space. They arrived, somewhat irritated, at the 'silver delegation' section reserved for special guests, only minutes before the meeting was due to begin. Tony Dann, chairman of the South West Regional committee, was on duty at the door.

'I took them along to the stand, praying that there might be two good seats available for them,' he recalls. 'When we got to the reserved section, the block was filled solidly right to the back. There was a single seat vacant at one side – and two in the middle of the front row!

'I asked the steward afterwards if he had held those two seats for someone, and he said he had not. I believe God had held them, knowing that I would be praying that prayer, but acting before I asked!'

When dealing with large numbers, little details assume considerable significance; that, of course, is a Bristolian tradition, the phrase 'shipshape and Bristol fashion' dating from the fitting out of old sailing ships in the city's port. The area designated for the workers' car park was occupied by six horses, resting from their labour of hauling tourists around the city in old fashioned horse-drawn buses. Anthony Bush had a simple answer to that one; he took them home for the week. He put the horses out to graze alongside the 160 cows on his dairy farm a few miles outside Bristol.

Jane Tucker and Martin Williams were also grateful for some special consideration. Saturday 12 May was their wedding day, and they had booked Bristol City's Dolman Suite at Ashton Gate for the reception at the very time Billy Graham's meeting was due to begin. With only days to go, Jane's mother discovered that there would be nowhere for the bride, groom and guests to park their cars. The Mission England office came to the rescue; finding a coach from somewhere they bussed the guests in free of charge.

The possibility of inconveniencing local people not attend-

ing the meetings was often on organisers' minds, in all the
missions. The proclamation of the Christian message should
be accompanied by practical Christian methods. In Bristol,
a team of visitors took flowers, a free copy of the pre-mission
introductory magazine *Billy Graham: the man and his mission*
and some tickets for the meetings to each household in the
immediate neighbourhood of the stadium before the mission
began. One resident later wrote to the local newspaper to say
that her street was kept cleaner that week than for the other
51 weeks of the year – although it was the city council, not the
Mission England staff, who were responsible for sweeping
the gutters.

Building a road bridge and re-opening a railway line were
only two of the civil engineering projects faced by the South
West organisers. Inside Ashton Gate, stadium task group
chairman Bill Spencer and his helpers had similar problems
on their minds.

There was a large standing area in front of the Dolman
Stand (opposite the platform) running the length of the
pitch, and its floor level was much lower than that of the
stand. So the task group erected a temporary bank of seats
over the standing area. They built the scaffold structure so
that its top row came against the lowest tier of the Dolman
Stand, and therefore not only provided 2,500 more seats with
an excellent view but also gave enquirers in the stand above a
short cut to the pitch when Billy Graham invited people to go
forward.

In all, that meant 10,000 extra seats had to be found, and
shipped to the stadium. A local farmer, Michael Spratt,
bought a jeep and trailer specially to help the mission. He
collected the chairs, mostly belonging to British evangelists
who conduct tent missions, cleaned them, stored them in a
barn, then transported them to Ashton Gate.

These alterations were done with the full blessing of Bristol
City Football Club, who had even gone so far as to re-arrange
their last match of the season so the ground could be made
ready for the mission. But in British law the club is not the
only arbiter of what happens on its property. The local

authority issues each public place with a licence which restricts the number of people allowed to enter it, depending on the nature of the event, the type of people expected, and the physical constraints of the venue, with public safety and emergency precautions in mind. Because of the much higher proportion of children and older people expected at the Billy Graham meetings than would attend soccer matches, the local council approved a maximum attendance of only 25,000.

Mission England would have been happy with that number, but they hoped more would turn up. After protracted negotiation, they discovered that by knocking a hole in the back of the huge shed covering the terraces at one end to provide an additional exit, the permitted number could be raised considerably.

Again they had to bring in the scaffold contractors and build a staircase from the back of the shed to ground level. All that then remained was to find 50 temporary women's toilets to comply with public health regulations; British soccer grounds cater mostly for a male clientele. The task group had meanwhile also covered the indoor bowling greens at the stadium with hardboard and matting, so that the follow-up team had somewhere to work after the meetings were over.

In this respect, Bristol was unusual; there were less building operations in the other centres. But in each stadium there was always the platform to erect, temporary staircases to be built over the perimeter walls to allow access to the pitch, and, of course, the portable toilets to be hired and parked.

It was a huge operation, mostly achieved by a volunteer work force, and with a single purpose behind it: to make it as easy and convenient as possible for people to hear Billy Graham. For the members of King Street Chapel in Tiverton, a market town in the rolling countryside of Devon, it had all been worthwhile. They had taken six buses and a minibus the 70 miles to Bristol, and they saw 19 of their guests go forward at the meetings.

'I have been asked by the members to write to express our deep thankfulness to God for all that you have done on behalf of his work,' the church's pastoral worker said in a letter to the regional office. 'Down here in Devon we feel a bit far away from the action, but without a doubt the blessings of Mission England have reached us good and proper!

'We found that the folk we brought were really impressed with all the arrangements and administration, and everything was wholly honouring to our wonderful God. For myself, I cannot imagine how you all managed to work together so hard and so long.'

Prayer power

Had the Bristol organisers relied on manpower alone they most likely would have failed. People who had never met each other before found an ability to work together which owed more to their common Christian faith than their human willingness to help. Throughout the preparatory period, Anthony Bush and his helpers were conscious of a far greater power pervading their work. In a radio interview he once said, 'We've been living, in a sense, on our knees.'

Hilary Field, who left a lucrative job as secretary to the managing director of a large chemical company to become assistant to Anthony Bush, recalls that 'every time we prayed, the Lord sent someone through the door' who could take over some urgent task – like sending out 40,000 regional newsletters.

When she first saw the regional office, Hilary Field went home and cried. Water was running down the inside walls, the wind was howling through it 'like Wuthering Heights', and the warm acrid smell of a nearby brewery hung in the air. Becket Hall was part of a disused church in Bristol's commercial district, one of three within a short walk of each other reduced to empty shells either by wartime bombing or when old residential property disappeared in redevelopment schemes.

Anthony Bush insisted on laying carpets, but there was no money for furniture. So Roger Lilley, the bus park organiser, set out to canvas local businesses for spare items which

Mission England could borrow. It was not long before he met a senior manager in a large insurance company who took him to the second floor of an office block. It was full of furniture the company would not need for another two years – the time Mission England required it for. And when volunteers humped it down to Becket Hall, they found the shelving units exactly fitted the alcoves.

Another answer to prayer came two years before the stadium mission, when the contract was signed with Bristol City Football Club. The Fourth Division Club, in a financially difficult phase, needed the full amount of the stadium hire charge in advance, and Mission England did not have it. An anonymous donor paid the bill direct to Bristol City Football Club. (The South West also received financial support from as far away as the tiny British outpost in the Falkland Islands in the South Atlantic, where Christians asked for the video tapes of the meetings so they could run their own mission.)

As Billy Graham's arrival drew nearer, the anticipation of the region's Christians grew stronger. Jenny Hockin, who organised a bus from Cornwall, told a local radio reporter, 'There was a sense of expectancy in the air.' People who were not Christians picked up the atmosphere; a number of people who were counselled at the meetings spoke of having an awareness of God for some months.

So it was not surprising that one 52 year old man said as he invited Christ into his life after a Bristol meeting, 'Tonight it all jelled for me.' Nor, perhaps, should it have been so surprising as it was that when Billy Graham gave his invitation for a public commitment to Christ, 2,352 people went forward. They amounted to 7.6 per cent of the audience, the highest first-day response at a Graham meeting for almost a decade. Opening meetings are usually full of Christians observing the proceedings before daring to take their non-Christian friends.

It was also nearly double the normal response rate seen by the Graham team around the world, and it was to grow even larger to an average 8.4 per cent by the end of the week.

Either Bristol was unusual or Britain really was on the verge of a spiritual awakening.

Perhaps the biggest test came on Tuesday and Wednesday nights. British summers are famed for their unpredictable weather; and it rained. (Billy Graham once said that he found British weather forecasters much more accurate than their American counterparts. They usually promised the possibility of some rain, and the possibility of bright sunny intervals, and they were, of course, right every time. Americans, he said, tried to be too specific and were usually wrong!)

Tuesday was affected more by drizzle, but on Wednesday it rained steadily all day. Yet 31,000 people turned up and 2,262 went forward. People out in the open stayed sitting during the hymns to keep their chairs dry. Looking down on the mass of umbrellas, one local journalist wrote that the pitch looked 'like a bed of exotic mushrooms'. And much to the counsellors' relief the rain stopped in time to keep the literature they gave to enquirers dry.

That night was also one of the few to feature a local person speaking about his faith. The preliminaries were normally kept to 35 minutes, which allowed for a soloist or a speaker, but not both. Nigel Sharp, who had been working as the South West Region's press officer, told of the time six years previously when his marriage and business had collapsed and he had learned that he had the incurable disease, multiple sclerosis.

'I decided to commit suicide,' he said. 'So I stole some drugs, and bought some whisky with a cheque I knew would bounce. But on my way to the place I had chosen to do away with myself, I met a group of gospel singers.

'I don't really know what happened, but I found myself in a Cathedral watching a Billy Graham film, and it seemed to make a lot of sense. I didn't go forward, but I made a commitment to Christ the next day.'

Advised by a church minister to confess his crimes to the police, he soon found himself remanded in a cell. On the wall of the cell was written, 'Without honesty, there is no truth.

Without truth, there is no love. Without the love of Christ there is nothing.'

Next morning a burly policeman came into the cell to interview him. Nigel Sharp explained he had confessed because he had become a Christian.

'Then there's only one thing to do,' the policeman said. 'Let's pray about it.' After that, he spoke to the chemist, who dropped the charges, and he put money into Nigel Sharp's bank account so the cheque would not bounce, and he admitted that he had written the text on the wall.

The living reality of Jesus Christ struck many people for the first time at the Bristol meetings. A factory security officer told his counsellor, 'I am a church member but I have never had a personal encounter with Jesus Christ in the way Billy Graham said is possible.'

A rather damning indictment of a local church which had lost its spiritual edge came from a girl who went forward and who later spoke on a local radio phone-in. 'I do go to church,' she said, 'Sunday school teacher and that sort of thing. But I just never thought of it as actually being God. I just thought of it as being good over bad and that's it.'

It was not all church people finding their bearings, however. A 29 year old salesman went to Ashton Gate with a car load of friends, none of whom attended church. They all went forward to accept Christ. And a 17 year old who had no church experience told his counsellor, 'I had to come forward; they never taught me like this at school.'

Making history

The response to Billy Graham's preaching in Bristol was as symbolic as it was significant. Bristol has a history of gospel preaching and revival. The city is full of churches, and the first Methodist Chapel ever to be built in Britain is now a tourist attraction in the main shopping centre. In the eighteenth century George Whitefield preached in the open air to the miners of Kingswood, then a village but now part of the city's urban sprawl, and John Wesley joined him. In the nineteenth century George Muller founded his famous orphanages in Bristol, relying entirely on prayer for his income and despite making no public appeal receiving huge cash gifts for his project.

Billy Graham alluded to this history in his opening remarks at Bristol. 'God can do it again!' he said. 'And it could spread from here across England to Scotland, Wales and Ireland, and to other parts of the world. This is history in the making, and you are part of it.'

At the time – before he had even preached his first sermon in the city – it sounded a dangerous statement, one which could easily bounce back as a piece of unfounded enthusiasm. But by the end of the eight-day mission, with a total attendance not far short of a quarter of a million and a public response of over 20,000 people, he was not the only person talking about revival.

The West Country had a lot going for it, of course. That religious heritage has not completely died away, and there are large pockets of strong evangelical life spread across the region, with churches able to feed many potential enquirers into the mission meetings. One such church is Christ Church Clifton, its soaring spire as much a landmark as Bristol's famous Clifton suspension bridge, built by Brunel over the Avon gorge, which the church almost overlooks. Set in an area of mixed housing, where many of the elegant nineteenth century properties have been turned into student apartments, it has over 700 members, and it received over 230 referrals of enquirers from the Ashton Gate meetings.

Bristol is also a relatively prosperous place, with an unemployment rate lower than the national average, and it is set in a region largely dominated by gently rolling and very attractive countryside, a favourite haunt of tourists. (Some of the Graham team did their own sightseeing with a difference. Musicians Cliff Barrows, George Beverley Shea and George Hamilton IV went to the grey limestone cliff at Burrington Coombe where Augustus Toplady sheltered during a thunderstorm and composed the hymn *Rock of Ages*. The trio sang the hymn in the shadow of the cliff to a battery of press men – and in a light drizzle.)

Members of the Billy Graham and Mission England team were not allowing themselves to be carried away by the results in Bristol. As they motored northwards through a patchwork of fields green with the early growth of corn and brilliant yellow from the blooms of oilseed rape, they were heading for a more rugged terrain which was renowned for its high unemployment and its relatively low level of church life.

It had also been described as the graveyard of evangelists...

6

New life in the graveyard

Roker Park, Sunderland, 26 May – 2 June

'Could you tell me why you are coming to hear Billy Graham tonight?'

In the narrow streets surrounding Roker Park football ground in Sunderland, the one and two storey houses overshadowed by the tall stands, Mission England team members were conducting vox pop interviews. They were for broadcast to an American radio audience, but also partly for the team's own interest.

'Just to see what he's like. I just fancied coming down.'

'He's supposed to have something good to say so I thought I'd better come and hear him.'

'I don't know.'

'He's interesting.'

Three men and a woman gave their terse comments in an accent which transatlantic ears found hard to understand: gutteral, with far less lip-movement than speech therapists would normally encourage. But their comments helped to kill stone dead a myth which had troubled the Mission England team during the long diagonal journey from Bristol in the South West to Sunderland in the North East, and to explain a phenomenon which had taken everyone by surprise.

The myth was that people in the region were hard, insular and generally uninterested in religion. The phenomenon was that they turned out in much larger numbers than many expected, averaging 15,500 per meeting over the eight days of the mission. They also responded in greater numbers to the call for commitment than the people in Bristol; nine and a half per cent of the attendance went forward.

The North East knew the gospel, in its Celtic expression, long before Augustine brought the Roman form to the shores of Kent 350 miles to the south in the fifth century AD. When the Reformation led to the decline of the monastic orders, Presbyterianism took root, partly because of the strong Scottish influence coming across Hadrian's Roman wall. In the nineteenth century Methodism flourished in the region like a desert flower. Centred on the local coal mining communities, it declined as church members left the pits and moved away.

Apart from the burst of new life when modern Pentecostalism was born in the region in the early years of the twentieth century, church attendance at 9 per cent of the population had declined to less than the national average of 11 per cent by 1979. Furthermore, evangelical churches, those most likely to provide the necessary core of support for a Billy Graham mission, were thin on the ground compared with other parts of the country.

With only four major centres of population – Newcastle on the River Tyne, Sunderland at the mouth of the River Wear, Middlesbrough on the River Tees some 30 miles south, and the much less industrialised and ancient university city of Durham sitting astride the meandering River Wear – the regional committee could count on only 760 churches giving any kind of support, although in Newcastle for example over half the churches joined in the mission. Having aimed to train 4,000 counsellors, they achieved only 2,000, which in the event of the large response proved a woefully inadequate number.

Writing in the regional bulletin shortly before the Billy Graham mission began, David Vardy, a local businessman and chairman of the stadium committee, said, 'For too long now churches in our region have been on the defensive while numbers have declined and many buildings have closed. We are now in a situation where we can take a giant step forward.'

Billy Graham summed up the character of the region at the opening meeting. 'You're a marvellous, *hardy* people here in the North East,' he said. The environment is exposed to harsh winds blowing in from the North Sea, and the people have been long used to earning their bread the hard way; mining, shipbuilding, steelworking and chemical manufacture have been the staple source of income.

The smaller towns and villages are dominated by plain, angular churches and houses built in dark stone, reflecting, it seems, the dogged personalities of their occupiers. The spacious countryside rambles with rugged, although not bleak, moors and woodlands as fine as any in Britain, but the region is contained by hills on three sides and the sea on the fourth, reinforcing the natural independence and sense of community its inhabitants have. Hardy, independent groups of people are not always inclined to welcome strangers, especially those with a message of dependence upon God.

Nineteen ladies, most of them having little church involvement, were waiting in the saloon bar of their local pub in South Shields, a few miles from Sunderland. A bus from a neighbouring church had arranged to pick them up and take them to hear Billy Graham; one centre of the community was befriending another. Tape recorder at the ready, the question was put once more: 'Why?'

'He's been around a long time. He must have something to say.'

'They say it's quite an experience and you feel different.'

'I hope we're better when we come out.'

'I thought it might be interesting.'

Beneath the allegedly independent exterior lay a softer centre. There was in the region a warmth of welcome and a clubbishness which people from the south of England tend to believe only exists in storybooks. English independence has migrated to the semi-detached lifestyle of the richer home counties surrounding London, leaving behind in the north something more valuable than real estate.

The relative absence of prosperity in the region, paralysed

with one of the highest unemployment rates in Britain, was also, it seems, stripping some people of their independence and, in their naked helplessness, prompting them to search for God.

Hope is born again

Bob was brought up in Newcastle, the region's largest city, north-west of Sunderland. He was a 'lumper' in a lead works, stacking 100-pound ingots of metal into two-ton piles. Ten years ago he gave up his job through illness and his income slumped to a quarter of his old earnings. And he had just married and taken on four step-children into the bargain.

He remained unwell, and knew that there would never be any work for him: the jobs he could do were given to the fit and healthy at the front of the queue. With time on his hands, Bob began to read, especially books which tried to answer some of life's deep questions. Religious education had bored him at school (especially as the usual punishment for bad behaviour was to write out verses from Genesis), but about a year before the Billy Graham mission he began to wonder if there might be anything in the Jesus business.

The books he read agreed that Jesus existed, so it was possible that he really had done and said some of the things recorded in the Bible. Bob read the four Gospels and found they basically agreed with each other. But the resurrection was a problem for him. Some books had explained it away: Jesus was not really dead; someone took his place on the cross; even that the disciples ate the body. He found the ideas silly, but could someone really rise from the dead?

In June 1984, he went with five unemployed men to meet Billy Graham privately. Mission England organisers had arranged the meeting so that the evangelist could hear at first hand of the pressures and problems of unemployment in the region. Bob was impressed by him, and later went to one of the mission meetings.

He did not go forward. But one phrase stuck in his mind; Billy Graham had said that he did not know all the answers.

If *he* didn't, why should Bob need to? Bob decided to accept the Gospels at face value, and he committed his life to Jesus Christ a few days later.

'It changed my life completely,' he said at a press call later in the week. 'I can't explain it. I went as a sceptic and came back a changed person. I'd been looking and not seeing. It's really strange. I had no hope, then suddenly there's a light there.'

Bob still does not have a job. And he is still unwell. But his independence has gone, and in its place has come a new self-respect. His family go to church with him, and he is learning to control the frustration and bad temper caused by his illness.

Also at that private meeting with Billy Graham were Tony and Sid. Tony had been a thief and had not had a job since he left school. Having become a Christian, he had discovered that 'God is in control of my life and that everything will work out.' Together with the others he had joined a project set up jointly by a Newcastle church, St Paul's, Elswick, and the Toc H organisation, and found he could do useful, although unpaid, work in the community. (Two of the six men were in fact too busy to attend the press call – working voluntarily at the stadium preparing for the mission meeting that evening.)

Sid had become a Christian while working at an armaments factory. Like Bob, he had to leave work for health reasons, in his case with a slipped disc. He had been through a government-sponsored re-training programme, but had been in and out of jobs.

'At times when it's black,' he said, 'there's a peace which floods into one's being. Most people go through life looking through an eight-millimetre camera. When Jesus comes into your life he gives a cinemascope perspective.'

That meeting with Billy Graham was two-sided. Frequently during the summer the evangelist was to look back to it and tell audiences in other parts of the country that unemployed Christians might not get jobs, but that they had inner resources to cope with the situation.

'My heart goes out to those who are unemployed,' he said at the opening press conference in Sunderland. 'They shouldn't feel second rate citizens. Everyone is made in the image of God. All have dignity. All need forgiveness – ourselves and those who have offended us. There's a spiritual rest which a person can have even during an economic crisis. We can develop the spiritual side of our nature whether we have a job or not.'

He made it clear, however, that Christians could not be passive in the face of social need. 'Christians should be involved in political action. They should take stands on things, but they won't always agree. No one person speaks for the whole church. We are to take a stand on moral issues in the social arena – race, war and peace, poverty – and do something about it. Love is an active word.'

The Elswick project itself revealed that biblical blend of spiritual and physical concern. The curate of St Paul's was one of the region's Mission England training team, leading courses on church growth and nurturing converts.

And the regional office began (and ended, after the mission) in a church hall in a Durham mining village where the vicar, Ray Skinner, had a workshop project and a welfare work. He was also secretary to the regional committee, and in effect the regional co-ordinator for the first year. During the Billy Graham phase, the church hall roof blew off, and another church which had been earmarked as an overflow office was damaged in the same storm. But in another miracle of timing, a Christian businessman offered the region the use of spacious offices above his hypermarket.

Someone else who knew what it was to be without a job, and who could speak the language of North East men, was Dave Merrington. He had been assistant manager of the Sunderland Football Club, and his return to Roker Park during the Wednesday meeting was greeted with cheers. But he had come to talk about Christ, not soccer.

He told the largest crowd of the week, 20,363, that becoming a Christian was 'the best and most important decision I've ever made in my life.' Christ, he said, was a real man, tough as the nails which pinned him to the cross, and not the 'weak and insipid marshmallow which he is sometimes portrayed as by the world'. Being a Christian can be tough he added, but 'Christ will love you and stick to you through good times and bad.'

The myths are buried

Nineteen year old Joanna Thorne, also a sports lover, but hailing from the south of England, had already proved the truth of Dave Merrington's words. On the Monday night she told the audience of the day when all her dreams were shattered. When she was 16 she discovered she had bone cancer and that she might lose her leg, and never play hockey again. It was a topical subject. British TV newscaster Reginald Bosanquet had died a few days previously from cancer; fresh, too, in Christian memories, were the recent deaths of American writer Francis Schaeffer and British evangelist David Watson from the same disease.

Joanna Thorne cried out to God, 'I know I love you. I pray your will be done. But you've got to help me. I'm so scared.'

Her leg was amputated, and she underwent a period of chemotherapy. The cancer spread to her lungs and she had two more operations. Clear of the disease now, she looked back and said, 'The Lord carried me through.'

Her clear voice, quavering a little at the beginning through her natural nervousness, helped many of the 10,766 people present – the lowest attendance at any meeting during the summer – to forget the bitterly cold wind sweeping off the sea and across Roker Park.

Billy Graham preached that night to young people. 'Life doesn't make sense to young people,' he said. 'They're looking for something to believe in.' No doubt with Joanna Thorne's testimony in mind, he said 'The Holy Spirit gives you power to do things you couldn't normally do, and to resist the things that are wrong.'

When he gave the invitation, 14.5 per cent of the people in the stadium went and stood in front of the platform. It was the highest response of the summer, the highest ever seen at a Billy Graham meeting in Britain, and perhaps the highest seen by the Graham team anywhere in the world. And it occurred on the coldest late spring bank holiday on record: the temperature during the evening on 28 May 1984 fell to 5°C (41°F), and the wind was gusting over the cliffs a short distance from the stadium at 20 miles an hour.

After only three meetings, the myths had been buried and there was no possibility of them being resurrected. God had not left the North East in the cold, even if the economic climate had left in frozen silence many of the region's once busy shipyards and smoky steelworks. But it left unanswered the perennial question: why? Why, when churches had been struggling for years, some making only slow headway and others being sent into retreat, did an eight day mission achieve such a high response?

It cannot be put down to men and money. Of all the Mission England regions, the North East was probably the most homespun; its budget was lower than the others and the committee bent over backwards to economise. Ostentation would not have gone down well on Tyneside; besides, the Christians were as poor as their neighbours.

That is not to say that the organisation was slipshod; far from it. The transport task group leader, Gerald Griffin, for example, decided to offer the economical facility of booking buses centrally. He and his helpers ordered 1,600 vehicles, at a total cost of over £53,000.

Centralisation had its problems, especially when churches changed their requirements at the last minute, or did not pay their bills in advance. And at 10.00 a.m. on the first Saturday the bus company told Gerald Griffin that they were 24 buses short for the evening run. By 6.30 p.m. they had enough. 'I think it showed to those arranging the buses that having faith can move mountains,' he said.

In one respect, however, the North East had led the rest. A year before the Billy Graham phase, two Church of England curates, Kerry Thorpe from Chester-le-Street, near Durham, and Tony Adamson from Elswick in Newcastle, were officially seconded by their dioceses to work half-time for Mission England. Apart from indicating the perhaps surprising measure of support for the project in an area where evangelicals do not predominate in the Church of England, their presence gave the region a far stronger emphasis on training than others achieved with the same materials but less manpower.

Kerry Thorpe had been a jockey and an undertaker and embalmer before becoming a minister partly as a result of hearing Billy Graham at SPREE 73, a large youth event in London in 1973. Tony Adamson had become a Christian in Newcastle at a TV relay of Billy Graham's week-long mission at Earls Court, London, in 1967. Between them they led 40 *Is my church worth joining?* courses and over 70 *Caring for new Christians* courses. (In one of the *Caring for new Christians* classes, Tony Adamson found himself teaching the man who had been his vicar when he was first converted 17 years ago!)

Looking back on those classes, Kerry Thorpe says, 'It seems we were able to equip Christians with a skill and then give them a context in which to use it. It was the conjunction of these two factors that proved so effective.'

Tony Adamson adds, 'The main lesson is that people will work together when there is a common goal.' From the training and motivation, there came also a new sense of unity among the churches of the region. Theological extremes associated with some denominations had perhaps widened the gap between individual churches unnecessarily. They discovered as they sat together through committees and training classes, that not all their suspicions were justified. Many churches slowly came out of their corners and joined forces for the mission.

Theological controversy may however have played a minor role in the attendance. Shortly before the mission was due to begin, the Bishop-designate of Durham, Professor David Jenkins, had apparently denied the virgin birth and resurrection of Jesus. (He later clarified his position by affirming his belief in the incarnate and risen Christ, but said he did not think that literal belief in the empty tomb was essential to

Christian faith.)

Billy Graham refused to be drawn into the controversy in Sunderland, or anywhere else as it simmered on during the summer. He did affirm his own belief 'in the bodily resurrection of Jesus Christ, the virgin birth, and that the Bible is the inspired word of God.' His suggestion that clergy with doubts should keep them to themselves was the closest he came to commenting on the matter; the discipline of bishops was a matter for the Archbishops, not for him as a visiting American, he said.

But at least one local minister noticed that the Bishop-designate's remarks had thrown his congregation into confusion and made many of them want to hear Billy Graham. 'They are saying they want to know if there is a word from the Lord,' he told a Mission England team member who preached at his church. It was a 'high' Anglican church, theologically rather different to many of the supporting fellowships; about 80 people went to hear Billy Graham from it.

Training, unity, and searching (coupled with the growing realisation that materialism was a spent force), all undergirded with the prayers of many people; these perhaps are some of the factors behind the unexpected response in Sunderland, which is the Mission England story in microcosm.

Stepping out in faith

Back in the pub in South Shields, the 19 ladies reviewed their trip to hear Billy Graham.

'I'm glad I went. I've enjoyed it.'

'I didn't. I was bored. He depressed everybody. Most people round here are on the dole. At 40 you're finished. They want cheering up. There's fights here every day. Religion's not going to change it.'

'I was cold, and I couldn't care less. It was lovely. Had I been a younger person I'd have just burned my boats and gone forward. But when you're 71 you just hope for the best. I was saying the prayer, but not to impress anyone.'

'He's very powerful. He puts his point over very powerfully. Yes, I think he's right, but it's something you don't like to think and talk about.'

One prayer in the seats, and later another lady committed herself to Christ after working through a booklet with a Mission England team member. It may not sound much, but it was a ten per cent response, although those two ladies, like Bob, will never appear in the mission statistics because they did not go forward.

Those who did step out in faith in Sunderland provided some delightful stories. There was the elderly lady who had shared coffee and sandwiches with her companion during the sermon to keep warm. When her companion got up at the invitation, she was heard to call after her, 'Wait, pet, you're not going to heaven without me!'

One 89 year old did have the courage which had failed the relatively younger septagenarian in the pub; she was a regular church goer but she said, 'Tonight for the first time Jesus has become real.'

And at the other end of the age scale, ten Christians in a school prayed about bringing their classmates to a meeting. A local church paid for a bus for them, and 47 non-Christians boarded it, laughing and joking about the meeting they were heading for. That night 40 of them went forward; it was a much different ride back.

But was it just a brief surge of new life, a spiritual flash of lightning, or an early sign of a spiritual springtime, like the first swallow winging its way back to a weatherbeaten, deserted nest? Many that week became convinced it was the latter; among them was Billy Graham himself.

'From what we have seen here already,' Billy Graham said halfway through the mission, 'I believe Britain could be on the verge of a great spiritual revival.'

On the opening Saturday, only minutes before the meeting began, a rainbow arched across the stadium for all to see. The platform at Roker Park was placed at one end of the stadium and not, as at most other venues, in the centre of the field. Behind the platform was a temporary bank of seating erected for the choir over uncovered terraces which, consequently, were not used during the mission. In front of the platform, in rectangular blocks, 5000 additional seats were put out on matting placed over the grass each afternoon; each night the chairs were stacked away and the matting rolled up to allow the grass to breathe.

The rainbow behind the platform seemed to rise from the sea and fall somewhere beyond the giant yellow supports of an oil rig in dry dock nearby. Many Christians, recalling the biblical symbolism of the rainbow as a sign of God's eternal faithfulness, were cheered by the sight. One person, however, felt that perhaps through it God was writing a fuller message in the sky for the eyes of faith to read, and her poetic interpretation of it did not seem so fanciful as the week progressed.

'I give you a promise as in the rainbow, that many will shine, strong and beautiful, and radiate my strength, such colour in profusion like blossoms of nature, and many will be drawn by their beauty. For many it is a beginning...Sadly for some, the rainbow is before their eyes, and then it is gone, and they could not see it.... Many have taken wrong roads which are but a false reflection of my glory. They must return to the strong root and have in me a new beginning.... Herein lies my promise to all men. Stand firm and be strong. Be rooted in me. Be filled with power. Be colourful, and I will bless you in all you do.'

For the preacher, one miracle of God's blessing in Sunderland in the rain was that while eleven team members needed treatment for colds and the like, he did not. It was more significant than it might at first appear...

7

The man and his message

When Billy Graham arrived in England at the beginning of May 1984, he had been unwell for some six months. In January, after a gruelling ten day visit to England, he had been immediately hospitalised on his return to America. He had a chronic sinus and ear infection causing him considerable pain. During his visit he had preached at All Souls Langham Place in London with the aid of a heavy dose of drugs, and he admitted at a press conference the day after that he was feeling rather punch-drunk.

During a mission in Alaska in March, his throat grew steadily worse, and at one meeting his voice fell to a whisper, then gave out altogether. Associate evangelist John Wesley White, a Canadian, took over in mid-sermon.

In the weeks before the Billy Graham phase of Mission England was due to begin, dark shadows passed over the faces of British and American leaders when they paused to think the unthinkable: what if the strain of 41 meetings (and countless press and media interviews) in a three month tour should prove too much for the 65 year old evangelist?

Indeed, Billy Graham himself had expressed doubts about the wisdom of the long campaign. During the International Conference for Itinerant Evangelists in Amsterdam the previous year he had suggested in off-the-cuff but public remarks that perhaps four missions would be better than six.

He was extremely tired at the time, and his comments took his own staff as well as the Mission England leadership by surprise. The situation was quickly resolved with no change in the schedule, and Mission England Chairman Tom Houston issued a public statement to allay regional fears. It put team members on their guard, however, and strengthened their resolve to protect Billy Graham from additional commitments on the days he had to preach.

His throat problem had not responded to treatment, and on his arrival in England a leading ear nose and throat specialist examined him. He ordered an immediate operation. It was simple and straightforward, done under general anaesthetic, requiring only a 24-hour stay in hospital.

Characteristically, Billy Graham was out before the 24 hours were up; he is a man of energy and enthusiasm. He had promised to preach the next day at Westminster Chapel in London, and he kept his word. He also kept his voice for the rest of the summer. The simple operation succeeded where months of medication had failed. He was clearly not at his best when he began preaching a week later at the Bristol mission, but he grew noticably stronger and sharper during it and the following weeks.

However, he had been ordered by doctors not to catch a cold, a difficult task for anyone given the vagaries of the British climate and the versatility of the common cold viruses. So he took extra precautions which helped endear him a little more to his audiences.

In Sunderland, the second stop on the tour, the weather was so bad that not only did he wear his overcoat during the meetings, but he abandoned his collar and tie for a red poloneck sweater, and donned a cloth cap with which the Geordies (the local Tyneside people) could immediately identify; it gave the evangelist the appearance of a common man. He also admitted one night to wearing two sets of thermal underwear, two pairs of socks and two sweaters, causing the presenter of a national BBC Radio magazine programme to suggest Billy Graham was preaching the gospel according to long johns. In warmer venues, a yellow V-neck sweater showed beneath his dark blue jacket.

Several times he acknowledged his gratitude to God for the miracle of keeping him fit during the three months. (He did have a minor intestinal infection between the Birmingham and Liverpool missions which kept him in bed with a high temperature for a couple of days, but did not have any major effect on his diary engagements.)

Over the years he has learned to look after his body, and although he no longer jogs or plays golf as he used to, he now goes for 'aerobic walks' several times a week. He is careful over his diet; he confesses to enjoying kippers for breakfast, but mourns the fact that he has to resist the rich cakes and cream he would like for dessert, in order to keep himself mentally and physically in trim. Away from home, he drinks water only if it is bottled, as a precaution against minor upsets.

Wrapped up with his overcoat and cloth cap he sometimes looked his 65 years, but in more relaxed and warmer surroundings, his hair still retaining some of its golden hue and his blue eyes sharp and bright, he looked much younger.

Family matters

Avoiding colds was only one of the problems Billy Graham faced during a summer which he later described as 'one of the highlights of my entire 40 year ministry.' It was not an easy or comfortable time for him.

During the Bristol mission he faced an unexpected blow; his wife, Ruth, who had been hoping to join him shortly, had been advised to have an operation herself. She had been troubled with a cough for 26 years, and it had grown so bad that she was at times in some danger of choking. Doctors said she needed surgery to restructure a hiatal hernia obstructing the valve at the base of her oesophagus. On the Thursday night in Bristol, Billy Graham got up to preach knowing that at the same time Ruth was being treated.

It was a larger operation than the one he had faced, and it took her some weeks to recover from it, having lost a considerable amount of weight. She eventually arrived in England in July, at the end of the Birmingham mission. Her husband was greatly relieved. The operation had been successful and the cough had gone, although Ruth, never a big eater, had lost some of her appetite. He had missed her tremendously, and even visiting journalists during personal interviews sometimes found him lamenting her absence. 'It is one of the prices you pay in evangelism,' he told the press.

'I can't stand a day without hearing her voice,' he often said in his sermons. They spoke on the telephone each day. 'She knows the time I'm standing up to preach and I know she's praying for us right now.'

To a great round of applause he once said, 'I love her 10,000 times more than I did when I married her.' He spoke of how they had met as students, a short while after he had broken off an engagement and in so doing had renewed his commitment to obey God's will in everything. 'I knew she was the one immediately, but it took her a year to find out herself!'

He spoke fondly of his five children and 16 grandchildren, and was clearly delighted that one of the second generation, Berdjette Tchividjian, still in her teens, was working with the back-up team in England. He explained her identity at one of the meetings; he had given her a warm hug and kiss in a relatively public place and he did not want his relationship with an elegant young woman to be misinterpreted!

Family life often featured in his sermons. On one occasion, in Sunderland, he departed from his usual practice and spent most of his sermon speaking about the duties of husbands and wives; more often he would raise the subject for a few minutes at a time.

'The husband-wife relationship is the highest form of communication,' he said. 'Broken homes are the number one social problem in the United States. The breakdown of marriage could lead to the destruction of our civilisation.'

'God,' he said on one occasion, 'performed the first marriage.' He spoke of the need for spiritual preparation before marriage, and that young people should realise that they are saying 'yes' for ever. 'Many young people get married and their expectations are too high,' he warned. People do not remain young and beautiful for ever, and no-one is perfect; there will come times when every couple have to admit their mistakes and work harder together.

He called on husbands to take back the responsibility for religious instruction in the home, which they had largely left to their wives. And as for the complaint that 'I'm only a housewife' he commented: 'That's the greatest thing in the world, to be a mother and a housewife,' reminding his audience of the responsibilities and privileges a mother has in helping her husband and children to develop their personalities and use their gifts. Parents should set a good example to children; 'Manners, morals and conduct are caught, not taught.'

He showed himself sympathetic to those people who had been through a divorce, however. A woman who had remarried and since become a Christian was unsure what to do. In a written reply to her question published in the programme at one of the meetings, Billy Graham said, 'Two wrongs do not make a right, and it is difficult to unscramble eggs, as we say. You say that you are worried that God will not forgive you. Such worry is unfounded for the Bible says that he will forgive every sin that we truly repent of. Another separation would only make matters more complicated.... Let the faithfulness of the future match the unfaithfulness of the past.'

And concerning single people, who often feel lonely, left out, and even embarrassed, he challenged the churches to be loving and welcoming.

Renewed strength

As well as being a devoted family man, Billy Graham also tends to be a workoholic. Always willing to oblige, he sometimes commits himself to a punishing schedule (although his close assistants filter the many requests to give interviews or talks so that the evangelist is not completely swamped).

In each venue he held a 45-minute press conference before

the mission, followed immediately by a series of six or seven ten-minute private interviews, and he admitted to being drained at the end of the morning. But he usually looked and sounded relaxed as he talked to a succession of people who in most cases he had never met before, and who in some cases were asking penetrating questions. Occasionally, as an assistant quietly reminded him it was time to stop for the next interview, he would say, 'O must we? I'm enjoying this.'

There were times when, because of the pressures and anxieties, he stood up to speak feeling tired and jaded. 'But I can sense the prayers of people,' he said, 'And all of a sudden it seems strength comes. I give the glory to God.'

His ministry was an example of how one biblical promise could be fulfilled in a person's life: 'Those who hope in the Lord will renew their strength. They will soar on wings like eagles, they will run and not grow weary, they will walk and not be faint.'

When he did take time to relax, as often as possible he went into the countryside. In Bristol, the first venue of the six, he was able to spend a quiet afternoon with Regional Director Anthony Bush on his farm. In Ipswich, the last of the missions, he stayed at a private hotel on the edge of the town, close to a field of cows. (To give him as much privacy as possible, he usually stayed in a different hotel to the rest of the team.) Each night he told the audience of his progress in getting to know the animals. He had been brought up on a dairy farm as a child, but the East Anglian fresians (holsteins to an American) apparently did not understand his accent and it was some days before they would eat from his hand.

But all through the three months he spent in England, he had more on his mind than his sermons and the timid English cattle. He was wrestling with an invitation to conduct meetings in the U.S.S.R.

He made no secret of the fact that he had the opportunity to go to several Soviet cities in September 1984. The invitation had come from the churches (he would have to use their buildings as religious activity was not permitted outside them), and it was known that no political barriers would be placed in his way. But he had an already full diary; he also had to face the consequences in the west.

In one sense, he could not win. If he went he would risk the criticism of having been manipulated by an atheist government for its own propaganda purposes. To refuse would be to turn down an opportunity to proclaim the undiluted gospel of Jesus Christ in a country where few other westerners would ever have such a privilege.

This may not in fact have been his major problem. Several times he told his English listeners that having once been to the U.S.S.R., and having been heavily criticised for what he said there, he still would not hesitate to return.

Norwich was one place where he raised the subject. 'When I went to Russia they said my visit would be used for propaganda. I said my propaganda is stronger than theirs.' The audience burst into applause. Billy Graham went on, 'They said the churches would be full of KGB agents. I said, "wonderful. They're just the ones I'm coming to preach to."'

After considerable negotiation, which resulted in the proposed schedule being reduced, he agreed to go there and the visit was announced at the final press conference when all the English missions were completed.

He is an optimist, he said. 'I'm optimistic because I've read the last page of the Bible. Jesus Christ is king of kings and Lord of Lords. There's going to be justice and peace in his kingdom. Capitalism isn't going to conquer the world. Communism isn't going to conquer the world. The kingdom of God will conquer the world, and we will reign with Christ. I'm looking forward to that day.'

Billy Graham never dealt with big issues like this without bringing them down to the personal level. 'Your greatest contribution to world peace,' he once said, 'and as a citizen of this country, is to give your life and heart to Christ.' The evangelist was never far away from the core of the Christian message with its call to commitment.

Basic message

'The Bible says'; the phrase which punctuates Billy Graham's sermons is almost as famous as his call to 'get up out of your seats'. But it was not always so clear to him. Like many other people, he faced intellectual problems after he became a Christian. He found parts of the Bible hard to understand; the claims of Christ to be the Son of God, recorded in its pages, were far-reaching in their implications. One day he just accepted in faith that the Bible was God's word. Subsequent experience proved to him that his faith was justified, that the Scriptures were trustworthy, and that the Christ they pointed to was ever faithful.

'I haven't had a doubt since,' he sometimes said, 'that my sins are forgiven, that I'm going to heaven, that Jesus is the Son of God who died on the cross for my sin and rose again, and is alive tonight, and that his kingdom will rule for ever and ever some day.'

Every sermon he preached was different, even when he repeated themes in several venues, and he touched on many topical issues. The core of his message always remained the same, however. He would point to man's need for God. 'There's something beyond science in man, and the Bible calls it the soul. It's 1,000 times more valuable than the body. You can please the body temporarily, but there comes a time when the soul gets hungry and thirsty. Without God you'll never find the satisfaction you're looking for.

'Suppose you had all the knowledge in the libraries, all the power of the world's leaders, all the gold in the world, all the sex you wanted. What would that profit you if you lost your soul? The soul must really be worth something if it's worth more than that – and Jesus said it is.'

That introduces a question faced by everyone yet usually receiving only half an unsatisfactory answer. 'Have you ever wondered why God put you on earth, what is the purpose and meaning of life? It's love. God loves, and he wanted people to return that love.'

But human beings are incapable of giving God the pure

love he shows to us. 'We all have a terminal disease worse than cancer that'll kill us morally and spiritually. Everyone is a sinner. Billy Graham is a sinner.

'God knows all your secrets. He knows everything you've swept under the rug. He knows those sins you committed years ago. He has it all recorded, as if on a great tape recorder, and it's going to be held against you at the judgment. God warns you: be sure your sin will find you out. What a man sows he shall also reap.'

Sin, in the biblical sense, is not what it is sometimes believed to be. It is not simply a matter of committing crimes, to which some people can plead 'not guilty'. 'You can be a murderer in God's sight by hating your brother, or by being filled with jealousy. You can even be a participant in the crucifixion of Christ. When you say "no" to the claims of Christ you help to crucify the Son of God afresh, as St Paul teaches. You and I were represented in that crowd that nailed him to the cross.'

But it is at the cross where the solution to the problem can be found. 'You are going to stand before a mighty God, but one who is a God of love as well as judgment. He loves you and offers forgiveness if you come to the cross. When Jesus died on the cross, God put your sin on him.

'God loved you from the moment you were conceived. No matter what your colour or ethnic background, God loves you. He can forgive every sin you have ever committed, including what is probably the greatest of all sins – religious hypocrisy.

'The cross in the Bible is not a golden thing, but it's rugged and bloodstained. When I see the cross I see how bad sin is – that God had to give his Son.'

The benefits of Jesus' death – God's forgiveness and the power to lead a new life pleasing to him – are not bestowed on everyone. We have to ask before we can receive.

'You must repent of your sins. That means you must be willing to change your mind and your way of life. You must come by faith. You cannot come by intellectual means alone, but by simple childlike faith receive the offer of forgiveness.

And you must be willing to let him take over control of your life as your Lord as well as your Saviour.

'You don't have to straighten your life out first. You just come as you are now. You don't wait until you are well before going to a doctor.

'I don't want to mislead you. It's hard to follow Christ in this generation with its pressures, permissiveness, violence and temptations. There could be civic, national, religious or even domestic opposition. Your cross is where you identify with the cross of Christ.

'But in the midst of it Jesus Christ will be with you and you can smile because there's a joy so deep you can't even explain it, and an assurance that you're ready to die. And if you're ready to die, you're ready to live.'

Billy Graham has always kept his message simple and basic. He attracts critics, mostly academic theologians, who accuse him of omitting half the facts. But he appeals to many people who are trying to find their way through the thick jungle of life's hard questions, and who need an earth-mover to clear a path rather than a guidebook to describe the tropical trees they keep walking into.

One such person was listening intently to Billy Graham in Sunderland. He had been a churchgoer for many years, but, he said, 'I've been having a great personal battle over the issue of becoming a Christian...a real and open Christian dedicated to the teaching of Christ.'

While in Sunderland, he met Billy Graham personally. 'I never knew that friendliness could have such a sharp cutting edge,' he wrote afterwards, 'nor that simplicity and goodness could cudgel us sinners so hard.

'But that's before I peered into the clear blue eyes of a saint, a man who has started to take this country by storm yet again.

'I defy anyone to listen to him and say they have not been moved.'

John Harper-Tee *was* moved. And the story which began for him in Sunderland continued in Norwich, the evangelist's next port of call....

8

Out of bounds

Carrow Road, Norwich, 9–12 June

John Harper-Tee is the associate editor of a local evening newspaper in Peterborough, on the western edge of East Anglia. He had travelled north to Sunderland to hear and meet Billy Graham as preparation for his newspaper's coverage of the Norwich mission, the nearest venue to Peterborough at which the evangelist would be speaking.

A fortnight after he had contributed a double-page report of his interview, John Harper-Tee told his readers: 'My own soul searching ended on Saturday night in the company of thousands of happy people when I took the decision to answer Dr Graham's call to follow Christ.' It was at the first meeting of the much briefer four-day mission at Carrow Road football ground, Norwich, on Saturday 9 June 1984, the day when some of his journalist colleagues were more concerned about another American, Ronald Reagan, who was visiting London.

Two weeks later he wrote: 'Since meeting Billy Graham in Sunderland, attending his Mission England meeting at Carrow Road, Norwich, and publicly declaring myself to Christ I have been overwhelmed by calls and letters from all kinds of people offering me their support and comfort.

'I would like to thank you all from the bottom of my heart and tell you that your words have been a tremendous source of inspiration during these first faltering days in my new life of following Jesus Christ.'

It was, he told Billy Graham, 'the most rewarding moment of my life, and ever since I have experienced a joy which I have never known before.' But going forward at Norwich was probably harder for many people than it would have been at any of the other five missions. The soccer pitch, looking at the time like a worn carpet with thin patches and gravy stains, had been re-seeded. Club officials refused permission for any one to walk on the grass; it had taken a pounding from over 70 games played on it during the 1983-84 season, and it needed all the time and help it could get to recover to First Division standards before the new season opened in August. Several thousand feet tramping on it in June would set it back beyond repair. The club had even decided not to hold any pre-season friendly matches at their home ground.

Consequently, the platform had to be cantilevered over the grass on massive steel joists, and enquirers who responded to the invitation to go forward had to stand on the narrow and dusty perimeter track. The path, having the deep red colour of the Colorado Canyon, was policed by counselling supervisors standing with their backs to the turf as enquirers came down from the tiered stands.

Faced with the supervisors' staring eyes and in a few instances aging dog collars, some enquirers probably wished it was a canyon and that the ground would swallow them up. Others, put off by the evident crush, were often heard joining in the prayer of commitment in their seats, but did not subsequently receive the literature and were not put in touch with a nurture group.

The regional committee had agonised for months over the problem, and even considered moving the mission to a large showground outside the city. But ultimately they felt it was right to accept the constraints, trusting God to work despite them. 'We were happy with the decision,' explains Regional Co-ordinator Peter Carroll, 'but sorry we had to make it.'

No-one was greatly surprised, therefore, when the response to Billy Graham's invitation resulted in just under six per cent of the total attendance going forward. It was the lowest response of all the meetings that summer, although still encouragingly high compared with the four per cent generally seen elsewhere in the world.

The attendance itself was not high, either, although once again no-one had known quite what to expect beforehand. The fourth and final day brought the first half of the summer's missions to a limp end with only 13,000 people turning out. Even the highest attendance, 18,000 on the Sunday afternoon, did not force the people in the cushioned area at the furthest end from the platform to feel like battery hens packed into tight cages; it was divided into sections by floor to roof netting to keep rival soccer fans apart.

But that did not make Norwich a failure. Local leaders here, as elsewhere, were thrilled and challenged by the response. 'Many churches are realising that there are such things as twentieth century converts!' said the East Anglia (north) chairman, the Rt. Rev. Timothy Dudley-Smith, Anglican Bishop of Thetford.

However, for some of the Mission England team, it was one of those weeks when nothing went smoothly. Setting up the final details, they ran into a host of snags; it felt like walking in wellingtons through deep snow. They were feeling decidedly jaded, too, Billy Graham among them. They were due for, and needed, a break.

The presence at the meetings of the devotees of an Indian sect which had set up a community in a nearby village was a powerful reminder that the battle here, as everywhere, was against spiritual forces as well as human factors. The statistical slump also became a reminder, if it were ever needed, that success in Christian mission is neither automatic nor guaranteed, even with a world-famous preacher topping the bill and 40 years' worth of experience behind the scenes.

There was plenty of interest in the region, according to a survey conducted by the *Eastern Evening News* shortly before the mission. It found that over 90 per cent of people in Norwich knew of the mission. Up to a third thought it likely they would go to Carrow Road, and 55 per cent thought Billy Graham had something worth listening to. The figures

While on a preparatory visit to England in January 1984, Billy Graham preached before the Queen at Sandringham.

VISION

Mission England was a three-year programme of local church outreach, with Billy Graham sharing in the middle phase.

In January 1984 he met the Archbishop of Canterbury and other senior leaders (left).

BRISTOL
Ashton Gate, Bristol: 12 – 19 May

Above: The crowd of enquirers was larger than expected and almost reached to the seats.

Right: Billy Graham, flanked by BGEA regional rep Greg Strand (right), and British policeman Billy Burns. Burns himself had recently been in the headlines after he was shot in the mouth by bank robbers.

Above: Youngsters crouch on cushions and shelter from showers.

SUNDERLAND
Roker Park, Sunderland: 26 May – 2 June

Billy Graham donned cloth cap, polo-neck sweater, and two sets of thermal underwear to beat the bitter weather.

Rain did not deter the choir (above) or the counsellors (below): Sunderland saw the summer's highest response as 14.5 per cent of the audience came forward in the wet.

Left: Counsellors were outnumbered by enquirers and had to speak to groups.

NORWICH
Carrow Road, Norwich: 9 – 12 June

Above: Because the soccer pitch had been reseeded and the young grass was only just sprouting, enquirers gathered round the perimeter track instead of on the pitch.

Above: Norwich is the centre of a rural area with a thinly spread population; but posters advertised the mission in most villages.

To protect the young grass the platform spanned over the turf rather than being placed on it.

MUSIC
Music featured in all the stadium meetings.

Top left: the BGEA music team; Tedd Smith, Cliff Barrows, George Beverly Shea, John Innes.

George Hamilton IV (above).

Soloists Sheila Walsh (above), Marilyn Baker (far left), and Cliff Richard (right).

BIRMINGHAM
Villa Park, Birmingham: 30 June – 7 July

People from the various cultural and racial groups in the Midlands sang in the choir and worked as stewards and counsellors.

Audiences everywhere contained a high proportion of young people, including colorful punk rockers.

Over 5,000 people, the largest number at any meeting, came forward one night; the stadium was filled and 4,000 watched outside on the huge Diamond Vision screen (below).

LIVERPOOL
Anfield, Liverpool: 14 – 21 July

The turf was protected by matting; there was barely enough space for the enquirers.

The choir gave Anfield's soccer song 'You'll never walk alone' new meaning.

Billy Graham took time off to visit 'a symbol of new life', the Liverpool International Garden Festival.

IPSWICH
Portman Road, Ipswich: July 24-28

Very few people could have been unaware of the Billy Graham meetings.

People came to the meetings from many parts of the world. At Ipswich, there were groups from America and Germany.

Fifteen year old Allan Paget went to Ipswich from south London and became the one millionth person to attend a Billy Graham meeting during Mission England.

compared favourably with the Gallup surveys taken in Bristol and Sunderland.

But despite that, there was a cultural challenge in Norfolk which had probably been underplayed and underestimated by the Mission England team. Railway travellers have an early introduction to the Norfolk culture. As their train approaches Norwich, the coloured light signals give way to the clanking semaphore type, controlled from a traditional signal box filled with heavy levers. Road travellers, too, soon discover that the place which centuries ago was England's second city has not followed the example of others of its size and importance by making big concessions to the motor car. All Norwich's approach roads are single carriageways, and the city was one of the pioneers of traffic-free pedestrian precincts.

Although a thriving commercial centre, it is full of narrow medieval streets and quaint old buildings, a quiet corner of old England which draws the tourists and provides them with a base to explore the flat fens to the west and the winding waterways of the Broads to the south east.

Norwich is an island of people set in a sea of green fields. The catchment area for the mission was predominantly rural and the population was thinly spread. Narrow roads and lanes link together tiny villages with fairytale names; Poringland, Stratton Strawless, Reepham and Swaffham. Whereas in other regions Mission England posters outside churches and inside house windows could not fail to be seen by hoards of townsfolk, in Norfolk the cows probably outnumbered the people who noticed the red and black announcements pasted on barn walls or fixed to telegraph poles. The region had only one fourth of the number of people the North East could draw on, one fifth of those in the South West. To fill the stadium comfortably, two-thirds of the 120,000 population of Norwich needed to pass through the turnstiles.

But there are villages where the churches are thriving. Church attendance in the region is higher than the national average. The Anglican church is stronger than the free churches, and is headed by Bishop Maurice Wood, who has been involved with Billy Graham since the historic Harringay crusade in London in 1954 which first put the evangelist on the international map. The Suffragan Bishop of Thetford, Timothy Dudley-Smith, well known as a hymn-writer, had also been involved in Harringay and was the founder-editor of *Crusade* magazine (now called *Today*) which was started by the Evangelical Alliance as a result of that mission.

In a tug of war the teams move slowly. In Norwich there were thriving churches (although not numerically large; 250 people would be an exceptional congregation) facing natural conservatism. The region was at one stage six months behind the rest of the country in its preparations for the Mission England programme. The vision of a preliminary year of training caught on only slowly; committees found their own and the churches' progress slow even when everyone was concerned for evangelism. Christians are not detached from their cultural roots and inherited characters when they enter the kingdom of God, but they are not always conscious of the effects of those traits on their ways and witness.

In Sunderland, an American preacher who could fill a football ground was a curiosity to be investigated, not least because he had come to an area largely written off by others. In Norwich, however, even allowing for the smaller catchment area, he seemed to be viewed by more people as a ship passing in the night through a region where time is measured in generations.

As the churchwarden in one country parish said to a Mission England task group leader, 'Our roof doesn't leak and we have money in the bank. What do we need a mission for?'

But every coin has another side. Another churchwarden, a titled man in his seventies, who had once been a Member of Parliament for some years, went forward at one of the meetings. His counsellor had some difficulty going through the routine of card-filling, because the man was so excited about being born again. He had been invited to Carrow Road by his son, who he believed had put his dad on a prayer triplet list.

He was not the only person to be excited by the mission.

Rural renewal

Ruth lives in a tiny village more than 30 miles away from Norwich, in one of the flat, low lying areas of Norfolk, literally off the beaten track. The nearest small town is several miles away. She was a counsellor at Carrow Road.

'When I came forward to counsel,' she said, 'I glanced round and saw that so many from our village had come forward – 18 in all. Four of these were girls from my own Bible study group. It was lovely to see one family come forward all holding hands.

'The Spirit is sweeping our village. One woman who I had prayed for came to know the Lord earlier this year. She brought two other friends to the meeting who both went forward. God is working a miracle here; we have a tremendous story to tell about the vision the Lord gave us for the village. The vision is growing, the church is beginning. Praise God.'

One of the regular features of all the missions was that people from considerable distances became Christians alongside the locals. In Norwich there was the American girl who had once been a regular worshipper at a drive-in church, but had lost her faith. She was working on a farm in Belgium, travelled first to London and then on to Norwich, where she found bed and breakfast in a guest house for four nights. At Carrow Road, she heard what she had been longing for.

There was a bus driver from Kent on holiday in the area. She had been searching for something to fill the emptiness in her life. At Norwich she realised that Jesus was the one she had been searching for and asked him into her life. A student from Hong Kong went forward; so too did a postman from Austria on holiday in Norfolk. One young man drove 120 miles to the meeting; 'I thought I was a Christian,' he said, 'but there has never been real joy or commitment.' A family of seven drove for two hours to Carrow Road so they could go forward together. The British, unlike Americans, do not usually travel distances willingly, except for holidays.

There was an Indian who went forward with her husband and son; she had first heard Billy Graham 15 years ago while a student in her own country. And another enquirer had first heard him 30 years ago but only at Carrow Road did the death of Jesus on the cross make sense to her; 'I've always wondered why he didn't come down from the cross; now I know,' she said.

Each venue had its own local characteristics, too. At Norwich, the choir discovered a deep unity together, and like the stewards at Bristol wondered if there might still be a corporate life for them after Billy Graham and Cliff Barrows had gone. Music was in the air at Carrow Road. One uniformed policeman patrolling the stadium was joining in the songs. And Deaconess Joyce Chapman attracted attention with her deeply expressive sign language as she interpreted for the deaf. What made her different from the deaf interpreters at other venues was that she brought along her little deaf choir. A dozen people all dressed in blue choir robes, sitting in the front row, were communicating far more eloquently than the heartiest soprano in the main choir, and making much more sense than those caught in the ritualistic rut of raising their hands high above their heads or plunging them deep into their pockets.

Norwich marked the midway point of the summer missions, and National Director Gavin Reid was looking back over the stories of changed lives, the cumulative attendance of 430,297 and the total response of 35,931.

'I wonder whether we have ever seen such a phenomenon in England this century,' he said. 'When we went into this venture in 1981 I was convinced that the time was right for Billy Graham's unique ministry in England. What we have seen so far has shown that the time was even more right than we expected.'

A lot happened in the four short weeks from the opening in Bristol on Saturday 12 May to the close in Norwich on Tuesday 12 June. The march of time had been logged in Britain's countryside as the oilseed rape had lost its luminous yellow sheen and the silver-green stalks of wheat had grown firm and erect. Now the hedgerow hawthorns were laden with clusters of white blossom like lumps of melting snow. June, although not yet flaming with hot sunshine, and still recovering from the bleak winds and showers of May, was bursting out all over.

In two weeks time, the team would be trekking to Birmingham, the heart of a huge urban area where even in summer leaf green appeared only rarely in a spectrum dominated by the greys, browns and blues of tarmac, brick and steel. But meanwhile it was time for taking stock and catching breath. Mission England had been discovering, and would continue to discover, some unexpected friends and some old foes in pulpits, studios and at newsdesks....

9

Surprise, surprise

Mission England was full of surprises. The *Christian Life and Witness* classes consistently attracted more people than had been catered for. The experience in Bristol, where 100 people were expected for a class and 280 turned up, was not untypical. Some 800 people became committed Christians through the classes, too.

The number of people going forward at the stadium meetings surprised even those organisers who had predicted a large response. Half way through the summer £50,000 worth of additional counselling literature had to be ordered because supplies were running low.

That could have put a strain on the £1.5 million budget, but giving had been good before the missions and offerings at them were generous. By the end of the summer the books balanced, and some regions had a small surplus to launch them into Mission England's third year of further outreach at the local level.

The Billy Graham phase had cost British Christians no more than £1.50 for every person who went through the turnstiles. Entrance to the meetings was always free, of course, but the actual cost, had people been asked to pay, was considerably less than they would have been charged to go through those same turnstiles to see a soccer match. Put another way, the cost was about £10.50 for every enquirer who went forward; in similar missions the cost per enquirer can be as much as £100, according to Mission England vice chairman, David Rennie. It was a surprisingly economic mission.

Not that a monetary value can be put on souls, of course. They cannot be bought; no amount of expenditure of time, effort and finance can guarantee a single conversion. Conversely, no figure can be considered too high for even one person to hear the message of new life in Christ, and for them to be encouraged to respond to the Spirit's prompting in their inner selves. It cost God the Father his only Son.

Media message

Something else which cannot be bought (except by corruption), and which must be earned, is favourable media coverage for any event or person, religious or otherwise. The British press and media have a scepticism which is sometimes healthy (in that they call people's bluffs who have no right to bluff), and at times destructive (when they approach issues or events with grossly preconceived notions). Furthermore, religion tends only to make the headlines when there is a scandal over clergy conduct or controversy over their beliefs. The churches may be as much to blame for that as the editors.

During Mission England that scepticism was not always suspended, but it was frequently overpowered by the same kind of curiosity which drew Geordies to Roker Park, Sunderland, and by a sense of surprise as well: the meetings were not as bad as reporters expected them to be.

Heather Clarke wrote in the *Leicester Mercury*, 'I went, as a Christian, expecting an over the top Hallelujah chorus and found instead a low key religious meeting with a few hymns, a few prayers, and a moving sermon from Billy Graham that was guaranteed to make everyone look deep into themselves and their relationship with God.'

Anthony Peregrine wrote a moving word picture of the final part of a Liverpool meeting in the *Lancashire Evening Post*.

'Not a tub was thumped. There was hush, calm and light and shade. The message was unequivocal, the messenger, now 65, is in no need of hysterics....

'In the old days there was an exhortatory hymn at the end to put steel into the souls of the unconverted to step forward. Now, there was almost a Graham whisper asking, beckoning, cajoling the doubters, the hopers, the newly convinced to leave their seats and make public their commitment.

'And forward they went, slowly at first but then swamping the 3000 counsellors...and all in an unworldly calm. Anfield had never been this quiet before, even when there was no-one there.'

The view that Billy Graham has changed became journalistic lore during the missions, although the evangelist always denied the charge. He told Peter Jennings in the *Birmingham Post*, 'It's a media interpretation. There has been no change at all. I probably don't wave my arms about quite so much as I did in the past, but that comes with getting older.

'I hope my arguments are a little stronger now and that I don't have to shout as much as I did. I haven't lost too much of the vigour I had 20 years ago.'

Perhaps it was the expectations that were different, based on stereotype and misinformation elaborated by imagination into legend over the years. Kate Jarnardi of BBC Radio York reported, 'I didn't find any emotion in it at all, it was just quite normal. He spoke quite normally. I expected him to be shouting and pounding on his Bible as I'd seen on television, but he wasn't like that. He just spoke quite normally and really came across.'

The *Daily Express* sent three cub reporters, who were in primary school when Billy Graham was last in Britain for a full-scale mission, to write 500 words apiece on the opening day of the mission in Bristol. They assumed that what they wrote would be subbed into a single short piece. Instead, the paper printed all three alongside each other.

Jane Slade, the youngest of the three, wrote: 'I was there to observe. But I couldn't keep it up. I wanted to be part of this fascinating union of people. I put my pen down along with my cynicism and allowed myself to become vulnerable.'

And Sarah Bond, who sang in a church choir as a child for the sweet money it earned her, wrote of being 'determined to have another, intellectual, look at the Bible. After all, sweets aren't everything.'

Rather different, and more enigmatic, were two editorials in *The Sun*, one of Britain's tabloids which trades off sex and sensation. On 26 June the paper said, 'What a wonderful bishop he would make,' comparing Billy Graham's positive and simple message with the reported doubts of some church leaders.

A week later it followed it up with a blast against a Methodist minister, Richard Jones, who had questioned the value of a Graham mission at the Methodist Conference which was being held in Wolverhampton a few miles from the Villa Park meetings at Birmingham. 'These past few weeks we have seen in Britain a remarkable demonstration of the power of faith,' it said, referring to the missions.

It was a strange ally to have, given that the normal content of the paper left little room for propriety or piety. But it no doubt helped to build a more positive media image of the missions which made it easier for some people to accept invitations to meetings. A reporter from another tabloid was asked by one of the team why Billy Graham was getting a more favourable press than in the past. 'Maybe after all these years we're just beginning to think he might have something,' was the reply.

This was certainly the view of some Fleet Street editors and publishers. Rupert Murdoch, owner of the vastly different papers *The Sun* and *The Times* called together about 18 senior newspapermen to meet Billy Graham over lunch. They were clearly impressed by his sincerity and the aims of Mission England. That put the project into the 'essential' tray of news and features editors, whatever they subsequently made of the man and the meetings.

More sober than *The Sun*, and in some respects perhaps more significant, was a brief editorial in the *Birmingham Post*. 'His visit to Birmingham can do nothing but good even if he leaves at the end of his mission with only a tiny percentage of the quarter of a million people expected at Villa Park among the newly converted. He will at least have caused the remainder to take stock of themselves.'

It echoed a sentiment expressed by John Knight of the *Sunday Mirror* in an interview published in January, when Billy Graham was briefly in the country. 'It is good to have Billy Graham around. For things start happening much for the better in ordinary people's lives.'

Rosemary Harthill, the BBC Religious Affairs correspondent, commented on the directness of the message during the Radio 4 programme on people who had gone forward at previous missions, *I got up out of my seat.* 'I think the most important thing about the Billy Graham rallies is not so much on their effect on people outside the churches but he does ask the absolutely crucial question, which is if you say you are a Christian and you believe that Jesus is the light of your life, he asks you actually what does it mean and how does it express itself in your life. And I think that's terribly important.'

There were negative pieces, too, and a good number where judgment was reserved; the surprise was that there were not more negative reactions. Norfolk writer George Target continued his longstanding argument about emotionalism in several papers and on Anglia TV. The emotion built up during the sermon, he suggested, and then when the invitation was given it burst out like a cork from a bottle.

In a radio debate with Mission England National Director Gavin Reid, he admitted that 'I am desperately torn. I am a passionate Christian and I believe that Christ is one of the answers to most of the problems, and so I am desperately anxious that the Christian message should be preached with power and fervour in the land, but I part company with Billy Graham because I don't think he is doing quite that.'

Church support

Similar mixed feelings came from the pulpit as well as from

the press. Lord Soper, the Methodist peer who is well-known for his open-air preaching in London, launched a strong attack on Billy Graham's 'totalitarian evangelism that uses phrases like "the Bible says" as if you have an infallible document from which you can read off what is required for a Christian life.' That was on Channel 4 TV; he made similar comments on local radio and in the *Methodist Recorder*, which filled the letters page for weeks afterwards with replies that were largely critical of Lord Soper's views.

After the initial controversy at the Methodist Conference when Richard Jones made his comments, the delegates voted unanimously to encourage congregations to support the remaining Billy Graham meetings wholeheartedly. The retiring President of Conference, Amos Cresswell, personally brought a word of greeting from Conference to the mission in Birmingham.

Much of the criticism within the churches centred on the apparent difference between a large meeting and the regular worship of a small congregation. One of the most outspoken critics was Peter Mullen, a vicar from Yorkshire. He said on the BBC TV *Sixty Minutes* programme, 'There's a world of difference between the sensational religion that you get from Billy Graham when you've got all these football grounds full of people saying "You're going to get your flipping soul kicked in," you know, and dancing about and carrying on alarmingly, and the sort of workaday religion of the ordinary parish church.

'It seems to me to be very presumptuous that he says that he knows that if the Lord came back today that he would be going straight to heaven. That's rather arrogant, isn't it?'

It was in marked contrast to the discoveries of sceptical journalists (and for that matter clergy) who actually went to the meetings.

However, the bulk of church reaction was supportive, even if at times equivocal. More than one bishop commended the mission by quoting C. S. Lewis's remarks that 'God has a habit of saving some people in ways that make me feel sick.' Over 20 bishops attended the meetings, and most of them had actively encouraged their clergy to support the missions.

The Rev. David Webb, Rector of Dunstable in Bedford-shire, some distance from any of the Billy Graham venues and only on the fringe of the Mission to London catchment area, spoke for many when he identified the strength of Billy Graham and the weakness of the churches.

'It will be easy for us to criticise – emotional, simplistic, contrived, etc. – but we are living in a country where many lives are being spoiled through lack of any sense of meaning or purpose. Many have no idea of God, yet desperately need to find him.

'One of the weaknesses of the Church of England (and of most other denominations too) is that we are not good at helping people find a living faith in Jesus Christ.

'So whatever weaknesses there may be in the preaching of Billy Graham and Luis Palau, let us remember that they are doing something that needs to be done…they have come to set an example.'

Typical of many reactions Billy Graham discovered per-sonally and publicly was the comment of the Bishop of Birmingham, the Rt. Rev. Hugh Montefiore. 'I don't agree with every word that he says, any more than he would agree with every word I say,' he wrote in his Diocesan magazine. 'But I recognise him as a good Christian man, who has been given by God a special charisma as a preacher of the Gospel, and I give him the right hand of fellowship.'

Other bishops had been more positive still. David Sheppard in Liverpool had fully supported Mission England and had encouraged his clergy to attend the training courses. In Ipswich, the Bishop of St Edmundsbury and Ipswich said on the opening day of the mission, 'The old false optimisms have gone. Men are looking for a working faith. We need the good news of the gospel, and my dear Billy we look to you to preach it to us.'

The respect and trust which Billy Graham had generated over the years, not least perhaps because his message was unchanged and that many who had gone forward in the past had stood the test of time, was rising to the surface. The churches were realising that they had a responsibility to take their message into the world, that their efforts at 'in-drag' had largely failed. They were realising, too, that in the words of the Bishop of Birmingham, 'This country is in desperate need of the Christian Gospel, and the essentials of faith on which we are all agreed are vastly more important than those matters on which Christians still disagree.'

They were therefore happy to throw in their lot with the preacher who did believe the Bible in its entirety and who believed that without faith there was no hope, in this life or the next. And the next stop on his English tour was to take him to Hugh Montefiore's own city, where amid the urban jungle only the Christian gospel held out much hope or comfort....

IO

The heart of England

Villa Park, Birmingham, 30 June – 7 July

Everything about Birmingham is big: the place, its problems, and its potential. The population of the city alone, at 1.2 million, is ten times that of Norwich where the Mission England team had been two weeks previously. The whole catchment area for the Midlands mission probably included 12 million people, many of them squashed together in the huge east-west conurbation of Coventry, Birmingham, Walsall and Wolverhampton, with the rest spread out across a huge rectangle of sizable towns and cities from Leicester down to Northampton in the east and Shrewsbury to Worcester in the west.

The area has a high concentration of people with non-European origins. Birmingham itself has some 45,000 with Caribbean roots; 29,000 Sikhs from India; 25,000 people from Bangladesh and Pakistan. Leicester, some 50 miles away, allegedly has the largest Hindu population in the world outside Calcutta. In some districts in the Midlands two thirds or more of the local residents are devotees of religions other than Christianity.

The stadium meetings reflected the cross-cultural nature of Midlands society, with West Indian and Asian people working as counsellors and stewards, singing in the choir and just visiting the stadium. It had not all been harmonious during the preparation, however, with some white churches making the wrong assumption that the predominantly black churches existed because they wanted to be separate, and that seeking to involve them in the mission was a waste of time.

The sad historical truth, however, is that some black churches in Britain were formed because their members received the cold cultural shoulder from Christians who would not accommodate their more exhuberant worship, or only grudgingly recognise them as both brothers and neighbours. (One church in the East Midlands did run up against a practical problem, however. They found it hard to have fellowship with the Chinese Church because its meetings were held at 1.00 a.m. when the take-aways had all closed down!)

Billy Graham threw out a challenge to white Christians during his Birmingham sermons. 'Get acquainted with people of other ethnic races,' he told enquirers one night, while speaking about the need to witness to others. 'Love each other. Invite them into your home. Show that Christ breaks down barriers between people.'

Once known as the city of a thousand trades, Birmingham had been a boom town making everything from jewellery to machine tools. It became heavily dependant on the car industry from the 1950s onwards, and now some 2000 companies serve the huge British Leyland works at Longbridge, like courtiers fawning to a king, and rising and falling according to their master's fortunes. In the decade since the early 1970s, those fortunes had been declining; the unemployment rate at 15 per cent is higher than the national average, and shows no sign of decreasing.

Seen from a distance as the M6 motorway slides down the sandstone slopes to the east of Birmingham, the city appears like a formless heap under a blue haze. A communications tower breaks the horizon, leaping skywards like a rocket on a launchpad. Closer to the centre, electricity pylons stand astride the elevated road, and copses of high rise apartments peer over its edge: people and their homes seem to be overshadowed by the symbols of power and speed, as if the late twentieth century has trampled them in its haste to find new satisfactions for old hungers.

'It's only in the time of this recession that the real spiritual needs have begun to be felt,' Canon David MacInnes, co-chairman of the Midlands region, said at the start of the mission. 'And I believe we have a bigger opportunity today than we've ever had for years. This mission with Billy Graham is tremendously important.'

And so it proved to be.

Questions and answers

It was a mission of contrasts, reflecting the diversity of the region. A Christian businessman flew a group of friends in by helicopter to hear Billy Graham. One of them went forward; he had made a commitment to Christ as a child but had never publicly confessed his faith.

An inner city church with a congregation of about 50 had 12 members visiting the local houses. They got 400 people to go on buses to hear Billy Graham, and received 40 referrals from the mission.

A former convict who had spent many years in jail for armed robbery also went forward. Something had been gnawing away at him, he said; he found out at the meeting what it was, and committed his life to Christ.

'I have a bit of a reputation for being a hard man,' he said, 'but one of the hardest things I've ever done in my life was leaving my seat and going forward.'

There was another ex-convict down on the soccer pitch after the meetings, too, but he was a counsellor. One of the enquirers he pointed to Christ was a policeman.

An articulate sales rep went forward, to be met by a nervous counsellor who led him falteringly through the steps of salvation to a commitment to Christ. 'You're doing fine!' the salesman reassured the counsellor several times.

A man from Nigeria came forward wanting to know that his sins could be forgiven; he was due to return to his own country within a week. A Punjabi-speaking woman told her counsellor that she wanted Jesus to be her saviour; at that moment a man stepped between them and forced her to leave.

For eight nights Villa Park stadium, dropped squarely in an inner-city area with a high density of non-Europeans living in the vicinity, was packed with people bringing their assorted questions and needs, and finding answers and solutions through the Christian gospel. The ground capacity was 35,000: on only two nights did the attendance drop below 30,000. On the Friday – the third anniversary of the invitation issued to Billy Graham to join Mission England – the gates were locked as the turnstiles clocked up 35,000 and 4,000 more people flocked onto the natural amphitheatre of Aston Park across the road to view the meeting on the Diamond Vision screen. That night over 5,000 people, virtually 13 per cent of the audience, went forward. By the end of the week the attendance topped a quarter of a million and the number of enquirers, 26,181, was over 10 per cent of the audience.

Birmingham had surpassed Bristol. 'It was the most humbling week of my entire ministry,' said the other co-chairman, Alan Boddington, an Anglican clergyman from Coventry.

It had proved Billy Graham's fears to be quite unfounded; in that respect Birmingham was like Sunderland. 'During the early preparations for the meetings here in the Midlands,' he confessed when it was all over, 'I thought we had selected a stadium that was far too big. People had told us grim stories about present day evangelistic efforts in the Midlands and their lack of success. We had been told we might even expect hostility or opposition.'

Indeed, the regional committee had at one stage considered hiring the National Exhibition Centre, a plush new complex in open countryside on the opposite (eastern) side of the city. It would have been more central for people coming from the East Midlands, and it would have provided a relatively small arena seating 12,000 people with adequate facilities for over-flows. It had disadvantages, however, not least because it was more 'up market' than a soccer ground and perhaps less appealing to some people, and the idea lapsed.

'Instead,' Billy Graham continued, 'I have found the most responsive and enthusiastic audiences so far on my tour of England. We are grateful to God for their positive response and for the way the churches of this region have worked and prayed together to bring this about.

'I now wish we had had a larger stadium and I also wish that we had planned to stay here a month rather than eight days. If a great spiritual revival and renewal takes place in the United Kingdom, I believe it may break out here in the Midlands. I have rarely seen people with such hunger for the simple proclamation of the gospel as here in the heart of England.'

There had also been a poignant and significant moment for some of the organisers earlier in the week. Those old enough (or well-read enough) to be able to look back at Billy Graham's three month crusade in 1954 at Harringay stadium in London were reminded that the number of enquirers coming forward after 23 meetings in 1984 had passed the total number who came forward in 70 meetings thirty years previously. As Harringay was seen as a turning point for the churches, not least because it gave new confidence to many Christians and resulted years later in a steady flow of men into the ordained ministry, what might Mission England therefore become? Billy Graham's words about revival and renewal were no longer sounding, even to staid British ears, like harmless exaggeration born of natural enthusiasm.

Crisis and coincidence

That Friday night attendance, the largest at any Billy Graham meeting during the summer, might never have happened if it were not for another of those happy coincidences.

Two days earlier, on the Wednesday, the gates had been shut some time after 7.00 p.m., and people sent to the TV relay across the road. One bus was even sent back home by police before it reached the vicinity of the stadium. Yet there were still seats available in the ground, and the cushioned and standing areas could absorb many more. The recorded attendance was 34,000.

It was the only occasion during the whole three months when anger and bitterness spilled over among the people going to the meetings. They brandished tickets and pointed to their watches as they claimed they had arrived before the deadline of 7.10 p.m., after which seats were no longer reserved. Usually, the good humour and patience of the crowds had been a powerful witness in itself to the love of Christ. One bus driver was so impressed by the behaviour of his passengers when the vehicle broke down that he went to hear Billy Graham and went forward to give his life to Christ.

A crisis meeting was scheduled at the stadium the next morning. Mission England leaders arrived there at the same moment as the Chairman of Aston Villa Football Club, Doug Ellis. They had not considered taking the problem to him, but as they walked together through the reception area, with its 'AV' patterned carpet and even the internal telephone in the club's claret and blue colours, they outlined it to him.

In a few minutes he was able personally to reassure the West Midlands police that the club was happy for the ground to be filled to capacity by the mission; the police, it seems, had been concerned that he might complain about the crush.

It was one example among many throughout the summer where Mission England organisers and soccer club management discovered a close and harmonious working relationship, with often more being given by the club than could ever have been expected. It underlined the truth of Jesus' words. 'Whoever is not against you is for you.'

In this particular case, the mission also did the club a favour. The only large area available for the follow-up corps to process enquirers' details was an inaccessible and unused space at the back of a new modern stand at one end of the ground. It was a long corridor, almost, created by the sheer shape of the structure between the sloping underside of the concrete tiers and the upright casing behind them. By adopting the now familiar (since Bristol) operations of knocking down walls, building a scaffold and board staircase, and fitting fire doors, the organisers opened up the space for their own purposes and gave the club more room for social functions or administration.

The one drawback was that the place was so dusty that a number of the night shift team went down with respiratory troubles. The cold grey concrete walls presented less of a problem; they were quickly plastered with hand-made posters. 'He who wants to enjoy the sunrise must live through the night.' 'Proverbs 26.14: As a door turns on its hinges so a sluggard turns on his bed.'

Friday night of the mission also saw the second appearance of British pop singer Cliff Richard on the mission platform. He had also visited Bristol, to sing and speak of the Christian faith which he had first publicly declared from the Billy Graham platform at Earls Court in 1966. (He had already become a Christian through the witness of a local church some 18 months before his Earls Court testimony.)

In Bristol he had said, 'I stand before you as one who cannot commend the Christian faith enough. Christianity is the only philosophy or religion which *demands* a response. If we reject it we have to be prepared to live with the consequences.' However, he assured the audience, 'Don't worry if you don't understand what the faith is all about at first.'

In Birmingham, he drew a spontaneous round of applause as he said, 'The one area of my life which I enjoy most is the Christian area. I've been a Christian for 19 years, and I still feel as if I'm new at it. I had a good time before I became a Christian,' he added. 'But a much better one after.'

Surprisingly, perhaps, for a single person, he also talked specifically to couples, saying that Christ could help cement and deepen their relationship. Listening to him was one young couple due to be married in a month's time, and they went forward at the invitation to start their married life with Christ building and bonding them together.

Training for evangelism

Another guest, who spoke briefly at one meeting but was present and not at all idle for the whole week was Leighton Ford. An evangelist with an international ministry, he was fresh from Southampton down on the south coast of England, where he had been speaking at an evangelistic mission organised in association with Mission England.

That, too, had been a fruitful time, with crowds averaging 5,000 for each of eight nights filling a large tent. The mission had hit local and national headlines after protests from local people led to a High Court ban on the mission using a large amenity area. It had been given to the town for 'recreation and entertainment', and although one legal authority reckoned Christian worship and evangelism was entertaining, the higher courts took a more sober view of religion and reversed the decision. The organisers had to find a new site quickly. When they did, it was better than the old, being more central and accessible. All things work together for good to those who love God, even if they do take a lot of time, tears and toil.

Leighton Ford, who is also Billy Graham's brother-in-law, spoke briefly of the death of his son from a heart condition and threw out the challenge, 'Are you ready to die – and to live?' But his chief reason for being in Birmingham was to lead a unique training course which took place at the stadium each day.

Twenty-nine young men and women, all of them practising evangelists although many of them doing other things as well, had been invited to spend the week learning from the experience of Leighton Ford, British evangelist Doug Barnett, and others involved in the mission.

John Wesley White spoke about sermon preparation, and Cliff Barrows on family life. There were sessions on the evangelist's personal life and the practical organisation of missions. They were taught how to train counsellors – and then sent into the stadium in the evenings to do one-to-one counselling themselves, something which microphone evangelists are not always good at.

'We hope that among other things Mission England will leave behind a band of young men and women with new vision and zeal to touch the nation for God,' Leighton Ford explained.

British evangelists have never had much encouragement from the churches. Only a handful are employed by denominations for an itinerant ministry, and few others have the status or experience to go it alone. It is a vicious circle; with few opportunities they can grow only slowly in experience, and without experience they will not be trusted with larger opportunities. Evangelists have in many respects been the Cinderellas of the British church, kept in their lowly place by the dominant obsession with maintenance rather than mission, of in-church activity rather than out-of-church advance.

The value of a large scale event such as Mission England is that, theoretically, it can stimulate churches to release people with evangelistic gifts which hitherto others have neither recognised nor felt they required. The aim of the school for young evangelists was to turn theory a little further into practice on behalf of the churches.

Two of the students, both Church of England curates, had good reason for wanting to encourage evangelism; their mothers had gone forward at previous Billy Graham missions during the summer.

And having strayed behind the scenes, it is worth staying there for a short while. The people working on the Mission England and Billy Graham teams were highly dedicated, professional people. They were also human....

I I

The American connection

Working 16 hours or more a day as BGEA media rep and press assistant to Maurice Rowlandson was something 31 year old Larry Ross enjoyed doing. At six feet, seven inches, he was the tallest of the team which more than once was described as a race of giants. (Greg Strand, BGEA rep in the South West, and Dan Southern in East Anglia did not, so to speak, fall far short of Larry Ross.)

But even though he had little time for daydreaming, Larry Ross could not forget the girl he had left behind in Dallas, Texas. On his birthday in July, while the team were in Liverpool, he proposed to her.

Being a media man he did it in style. He hired a 40 foot billboard in Dallas and got a signwriter to paint on it: 'Autumn Ellis – will you marry me? Love Larry.'

Autumn Ellis, aged 27, and a comparatively diminutive five feet eight, was taken by a friend to see the board under the pretense of a birthday celebration in Larry's absence. There was a space on the board for her response, and a can of paint conveniently to hand. She climbed the ladder and painted a huge 'yes'. Thirty friends were there to share the surprise, and they watched as she was also presented with three roses implanted in a watermelon – her favourite fruit – and an 18 carrot ring (yes, *carrots;* strange people...).

Autumn Ellis phoned her response to a friend on the

Graham team in Liverpool, and to arrange for Larry Ross to be awakened at 6.30 a.m. the next morning with a special breakfast in bed. It was brought to him on three trays, each of which had a vase of flowers and one letter of the word 'YES'. And the hotel manager joined in the larger than life engagement by putting up a sign outside, 'Autumn tells Larry Yes'.

There was a treble twist in the tale. The couple were brought together on a blind date by a mutual friend appropriately named Claire Love. Autumn Ellis's father, a missionary and evangelist who has worked in Billy Graham missions, will force his prospective son-in-law to look up to him; at six feet nine he is two inches taller. And just to prove that the papers do like a good story now and again, one of America's leading news agencies flashed this one across the continent.

Gentle George

Someone with a very different style and temperament was country and western singer George Hamilton IV. (There really were George Hamiltons I, II and III). He endeared himself to audiences in Bristol, Liverpool and Ipswich with his simple, homely and very unassuming faith and manner.

His only distinction in a crowd was the white embroidered 'IV' on his blue blazer; comfortable in an ordinary mackintosh, he ambled across the soccer fields after the meetings with all the time in the world for the people who clamoured for autographs or just a chat. He was happy strumming his guitar anytime, anyplace, as some of the team office girls found to their delight.

For him, Mission England was a memorable time. After Bristol he had to fulfill an engagement in New Zealand, and he seemed to be genuinely longing to return to England to share in some of the later missions. It was the first time that he had declared himself to be a Christian in Britain. He had often been on the European side of the Atlantic for country and western tours and festivals, but never before for a specifically Christian witness. As Earls Court in 1966 was for Cliff

Richard, so Mission England 1984 was for George Hamilton.

He grew up in a Christian home, and had always been active in his church. 'I've been, unfortunately, a closet Christian,' he admitted. 'I've been coasting along all my life. I wasn't exactly a Sunday morning saint and a Saturday evening sinner, but I felt my Christianity was for church and I could go my own way the rest of the week.'

Then he went to Eastern Europe and saw at first hand the sacrifices Christians had to make there. 'These people go to jail for their witness and here am I, a Christian living in the so-called free world where there are no restrictions on us, complaining about getting up on Sunday morning to go to church. That made quite an impact on me.

'I met people who are further along in their walk with the Lord than I have been and it made me ashamed of myself – and aware that I wasn't carrying the cross.'

A country song which he often sang seemed to be an expression of his own uncomplicated Christian faith; it sprang from his experience and became a prayer which many could identify with at the meetings.

> *Yesterday's gone, sweet Jesus*
> *And tomorrow may never be mine,*
> *So help me today,*
> *Show me the way,*
> *One day at a time.*
> *One day at a time, sweet Jesus.*
> *That's all I'm asking from you,*
> *Give me the strength to do every day*
> *What I've got to do.*

The coaching team

Someone who was very rarely noticed by the public during the missions, but who was often to be seen at Billy Graham's side, was a short quiet man called Bob Williams.

He was not, as some newspaper and TV reporters suggested, one of a group of American security agents. Billy

Graham had one personal security officer, who was usually also his car driver and always a British policeman who had taken a week off work to do the job for free. The others who accompanied Billy Graham were his close aides, and in some cases long standing personal friends, who took responsibility for the details of his itinerary and of the stadium meetings.

Bob Williams, at 34 years of age, was team leader for the BGEA staff in England. With red Indian roots, and a home in Atlanta near a mountain held sacred by his forebears, he had worked with the BGEA for 13 years in a host of countries, including Switzerland, Hong Kong, Brazil, Canada, Japan and the Netherlands. He moved to London, with wife Karen and baby daughter Stephanie, in July 1983.

Six other BGEA men also moved to England to become regional reps, advising regional organisers as they prepared for the stadium meetings. Blair Carlson, who had been commuting to England since 1982, went to live in Liverpool. In September 1983, Mike Southworth moved to Sunderland, Norman Sanders to Birmingham and Greg Strand to Bristol. East Anglia was served by Dan Southern in the north and Steve Huggins in the south.

Bob Williams described his role as 'coaching the coaches,' while he in turn was responsible to Walter Smyth. He too had taken up temporary residence in England, and was the International Vice-president of the BGEA, responsible for all Billy Graham's overseas activities.

In addition to the senior Americans, there was also a larger support team which moved with Billy Graham from city to city. Some people called it a roadshow or a bandwaggon; a few more disparagingly labelled it a circus. But unlike both roadshows and circuses, it generally kept a low profile, and its purpose was to organise and not to amaze.

The BGEA took responsibility for the actual stadium meetings. A regional Mission England task group prepared each stadium with the help and advice of the BGEA team member who had been living and working alongside them and the other task groups for up to a year before the mission took place.

When the team moved into town, they were usually accommodated together in the same hotel, and at least four hotel rooms were taken over for use as offices. Although at first sounding extravagant by British standards, where in some regions local Mission England offices and even their senior staff came rent- and salary- free, it had distinct advantages.

None of the regional offices could have found desk space for another dozen people in the busy and hectic two weeks prior to and during the mission itself. The team worked long hours; although the main team office was officially closed at 10.30 p.m., it was frequently in use much later, and other team members continued working in their rooms. That fact alone meant that cheaper hospitality with the team billetted out in local Christian homes was out of the question; they needed to be close together for ease of communications, and they needed to work anti-social hours. The privacy of a single room in an anonymous hotel also had advantages over private houses; team members could collapse on their beds at 1.00 in the afternoon and have coffee or even meals at 1.00 in the morning without disturbing others' routines.

In Liverpool, for example, the team list included more than 60 names. Only a handful of them were British; half a dozen senior Mission England personnel (including the triple leadership team of Gavin Reid, Eddie Gibbs and Brian Mills), and Maurice Rowlandson, the London Director of BGEA with some assistants mostly working on press relations and also keeping the other British functions of the BGEA running.

The other 50 or so people, mostly Americans, each had specific responsibilities. There were the long-term preparatory staff – team leader Bob Williams; regional BGEA reps Blair Carlson and Mike Southworth; Rick Marshall and Tom Phillips supervising the counselling and follow-up operations.

There was the platform and senior BGEA team – Cliff Barrows and Bev Shea; musicians Tedd Smith and John

Innes; overseas crusades director and vice-president of the BGEA, Walter Smyth; and some associate evangelists taking other meetings in the area. There were platform guests – the Agajanians, a trio, singers Larnelle Harris and Jimmy Mamou. A team of technicians saw to the stadium sound (Bill Fasig), sound recording (Don Feltham and Johnny Lenning) and video recording for American TV (headed by Ted Dienert). Then, of course, there were secretaries pounding away on word processors and typewriters, and people organising all kinds of tiny details (including the important task of getting Billy Graham from place to place on time).

It was rather like several orchestras. Each person had a clearly defined score and was responsible to see it was played on cue. There were several conductors; Bob Williams kept the back-up team playing to time, for example, and Cliff Barrows literally conducted the platform programme. Working as a kind of artistic director for the whole company was Walter Smyth.

Not that they always made a perfect sound; they hit a few wrong notes now and then. Briefing papers sometimes went astray; communications were occasionally confused. One of the reps had to change regions, from one where his inexperience in some matters could have hindered progress to one where it was irrelevant because the problems were different.

It all went to prove that they were human, but for many English people they were a godsend. 'On reflection,' said one Midlands region task group chairman, 'we could not have succeeded in our task without Norman Sanders' patient help and guidance.'

The 'on reflection' is important. There were at first some deep suspicions among some of the British. One regional staff member began his task believing that nothing good could ever come across the Atlantic, although by the end he was forced to admit that he had met some exceptions to his rule. Some British leaders had been fearful of being bulldozed into un-British activities by Americans who would never listen to local advice or experience. They found the reverse to be true.

'Extreme courtesy and tactful, helpful advice,' was one North East assessment. 'One always felt they were around as our servants and not our masters,' was another reaction, from the North West. 'One would not have minded it the other way but their courtesy and grace was refreshing.'

Not that the Americans had gone to the opposite extreme of being soft. Another North East assessment: 'They really sorted us out, got us organised, made us aware of the logistical problems involved. And they always began or ended meetings with, "You're doing a great job!"'

The British and American teams discovered a unity which probably surprised most of them. It was as though God was giving what retail executives are always offering: added value. The Americans did their job of helping the British do theirs. But in addition to the functional aspect, human friendships blossomed and spiritual fellowship deepened.

John Pugh, media task group chairman in the North West summed it up. 'By performing a highly professional role without ever losing sight of over-riding Christian motives, the Americans provided great spiritual uplift.'

And it was in his region, during the Liverpool mission, that some of the Americans, along with their British colleagues, had a rude awakening...

12

Earthquake city

Anfield, Liverpool, 14 – 21 July

Susan Pannell, an American who worked with the BGEA video recording and press teams, eased herself out of bed. She had had a late night; it was 8.00 a.m. and another full day lay ahead. As she placed her feet on the hotel floor and stood up, she suddenly felt very shaky. Her legs trembled violently, the room seemed to move and objects vibrate.

She sat down heavily on the bed, hazily trying to decide just how ill she was. After a few minutes she tried to stand again. Everything seemed fine. Cautiously, she washed and dressed, trying to recall the first fleeting seconds of consciousness and wondering how she could have imagined that the mirror had rattled.

Grabbing a quick breakfast and sitting behind her word processor in the team office, she kept her bewilderment to herself. Slowly, she picked up snatches of conversation, and a sense of relief eased away the fears. Liverpool had been shaken (but hardly damaged) by an earthquake, measuring five on the Richter scale but centred some distance away in North Wales.

It brought out the best in scouse (Liverpudlian) wit and the worst in copy-hungry journalists. It was an irresistable temptation to compare that so-called act of God with another which was currently taking place at the city's Anfield soccer ground. Out of an average attendance of 30,100 people at each of the eight meetings of the Billy Graham mission held here, 11 per cent of the audience went forward in response to the invitation to make a public act of commitment to Christ. It was to be the highest average response in all six missions during the summer, and by the end over 27,000 people had stepped forward.

It prompted another comparison, this time from Billy Graham himself. During the week he had visited the city's International Garden Festival, built as a tourist attraction over acres of formerly derelict dockland along the banks of the River Mersey. One of its features, the Garden of Hope, had been sponsored by the area's council of churches.

'When I came here,' he said in the local evening newspaper, the *Liverpool Echo*, 'I was told that hope was wearing thin on Merseyside, and a cloud of despair was thickening over the city.

'But the Garden Festival with its Garden of Hope, with the water bubbling from the rock representing the new life of Jesus Christ, is a marvellous visual aid for what we have been preaching at Anfield.

'Certainly the problems you face are enormous,' he went on. But the response at the mission 'tells me that deep down the people of Liverpool know that their problems are not just physical, economic or political. They are spiritual too…. My chief prayer for this great city and all its people is that they may know the spiritual resurrection to which the Garden Festival points.'

No one could doubt that the city needed it. Liverpool almost looks in places as though an earthquake has hit it. There are broad areas of redevelopment, hugh blocks of apartments sprouting from grass-covered slopes, cheek-by-jowel alongside rows of battered old cottages, all looking down towards the redundant shipyards and docks which litter both banks of the Mersey. It shoulders, like Sunderland and Birmingham, some of the greatest economic and social problems in Britain. Almost exactly three years before the Billy Graham mission it was the scene of some of Britain's most violent riots to date. Toxteth, a particularly run-down area just south of the city centre, had exploded with anger and frustration at the high unemployment and deep-rooted helplessness which anchored the racially-mixed area to the reef of poverty.

The myths of materialism had clearly begun to fade. In a Gallup Poll held shortly before the mission, 72 per cent of those questioned said unemployment was the main problem people faced. Second on the list was the breakdown of law and order, with drug taking, problems with the young and alcoholism coming close behind – issues which had not been mentioned in the surveys conducted in Bristol, Birmingham and Sunderland.

The cheerful optimism of the 1960s, captured by Liverpool's most famous offspring, The Beatles, in their song *All you need is love,* had proved unfounded. Were the group still together, *Eleanor Rigby* would continue to strike a chord of recognition in many Merseyside hearts:

> *All the lonely people;*
> *Where do they all come from?*

One church close to Anfield discovered to its intense surprise just how strong the spiritual hunger had grown. They had ordered 100 tickets for one Billy Graham meeting, and had arranged transport for the couple of miles' journey. Over 130 people turned up, and at least 30 of them were entirely non-church people who had come without warning.

Like any other Mission England region, however, the North West did not consist only of its host city. Geographically the largest of all the regions, it stretched down from the poet Wordsworth's former haunts among the lonely cloud-capped hills of the English Lake District, to the more rugged grey mountains and jagged slate quarries of Snowdonia in North Wales. Every night fleets of buses drove in from Preston, Manchester and the Lancashire cotton towns of Burnley and Blackburn to hear Billy Graham.

It took in more prosperous areas, such as the historic city of Chester, its streets lined with majestic half-timbered houses dating from the sixteenth and seventeenth centuries. The regional office was located in a quiet village on the Wirral peninsular, a tongue of land sticking out between the Mersey and Dee river estuaries. A short distance from the office there were signs beside the road: 'No horse riding on the grass verges.'

The office itself, however, had seen better days. A former vicarage converted into curates' flats, the church had declared it unfit for its staff to inhabit. But the Mission England team needed work space with a roof, not a home with mod cons, and they gratefully accepted it. Once again, availability and need had coincided with perfect timing.

The Christian leadership in Liverpool had taken to heart the deep spiritual and physical needs of the city. Unlike the North East, the region has for long had a vigorous church life and within it a strong evangelical voice. Toxteth and Everton (another area of great social need with a high density of population in post-war estates) both have evangelical churches concerned for evangelism within the context of community care.

Giving a powerful lead in that ministry has been the Rt. Rev. David Sheppard, Bishop of Liverpool. Formerly warden of the now famous Mayflower Centre in London's East End, he was a firm supporter of the Billy Graham mission; he had also recently delivered the annual BBC TV Dimbleby Lecture outlining the plight and powerlessness of people in inner city areas.

David Sheppard had formed a close working friendship with Roman Catholic Archbishop Derek Warlock. Over several years they had gained trust and respect in the community and had helped to generate a little sanity, restraint and hope where once those virtues had appeared to be fleeing the nest. They had also helped forward the slow healing process in Britain's biggest sectarian division outside Northern Ireland.

· Local Liberal MP David Alton, who visited one of the mission meetings which he described as 'a moving experience and of great spiritual benefit', spoke also of the church unity which it achieved.

'It has demonstrated so well what has happened in Liverpool during the last decade. I can remember when sectarian schisms rocked the religious harmony in the city, but the friendship which has grown up between (the two bishops) has brought about one of the most profound changes in Liverpool.'

It was a controversial relationship, however, and treated with suspicion by some evangelicals, especially those in some free churches, who felt that Sheppard was betraying his spiritual heritage by such close links with a Roman Catholic. The matter came to something of a head for Mission England when Archbishop Derek Warlock encouraged his priests to lead their flocks to Anfield to hear Billy Graham.

Theological minefield

Each night during the Liverpool mission, a group of demonstrators from a Protestant organisation gathered in the central reservation of a dual carriageway near the soccer stadium. They handed out leaflets and held banners. Two of the slogans were: 'Billy Graham does not preach the blood of Christ' and 'Billy Graham is sending people back to Rome.'

The evangelist probably did not see the banners; he entered Anfield by a different route. But one night he did preach very explicitly on the blood of Christ. Quoting as always from the Authorised (King James) Version of the Bible, a tradition he shared with the protesters, he stressed that the death of Jesus on the cross was the only means on offer for a person to receive God's forgiveness and to enter the kingdom of heaven.

That incident illustrated the theological minefield which the Mission England organisers had to pick their way through. The Catholic issue was more sensitive in Liverpool than elsewhere in the country because local feelings run high (the pre-mission press conference was held on the same day as Liverpool's annual Orange Day parade of Protestant organisations); it was not however absent in other regions.

The problem is complicated by differing views of the contemporary Roman Catholic Church in Britain. Some view it as rigidly unreformed as it was before Calvin and Luther shook it up in the sixteenth century, because its formularies are unchanged. Others view it pragmatically and see signs of spiritual renewal and biblical life and worship among some of its priests and parishes; they see a gradual, grassroots reformation taking place, rather than a sudden reversal of official views.

This put Mission England under pressure from both sides. On the one hand there were Roman Catholics who wanted to come to the meetings and bring their friends and neighbours to hear the gospel proclaimed in all its simplicity. On the other hand there were Protestants who could not co-operate with members of a church which officially held a concept of how a person became and remained a Christian different to that upon which Billy Graham's own message was based.

A third complicating factor, but one which in fact led to a positive way forward, was that all the main denominations were theologically mixed, as the controversy over the Bishop of Durham's views during the mission periods made clear. Views akin to traditional Catholicism were to be found among some members of the Church of England. Views which both Catholics and evangelicals would repudiate, ranging from anaemic universalism to revolutionary radicalism, had pervaded every church.

One thing was clear from the beginning. Roman Catholics who wished to organise buses and attend the meetings would be as welcome as Anglicans and Methodists, and anyone else. As Gavin Reid explained, 'You cannot have a nationwide project preaching the gospel freely to all who wish to hear it, and then keep one group out.'

More problematic was the matter of referring enquirers to churches, but this was where the denominational mix pointed the way. No-one was referred to any church, but only to nurture groups led by people who had been trained on the Mission England *Caring for new Christians* course. Most nurture groups were attached to churches, but others were interdenominational neighbourhood groups.

If there was a suitable nurture group of the enquirer's own denominational preference, he or she was referred to that. Mission England had always declared that it had no intention to steal sheep from one pen and transfer them to another. But it had also recognised – and denominational leaders tended to agree – that not every church, even within the Protestant mainstream, would be helpful to a person who had gone forward at a Billy Graham meeting.

Therefore, where no suitable church nurture group existed, in which the enquirer could learn more of the basics of the Christian faith in the company of sympathetic people, he or she was referred to a neighbourhood nurture group. After that period of initial follow-up, the enquirers were of course at perfect liberty to link up with whatever local church they wished; the nurture group merely gave them time to find their spiritual feet. Another of the Liverpool protesters' banners, 'Billy Graham is sending people back to Rome' was unfounded. It would have been equally untrue if 'Canterbury' had replaced 'Rome'.

The debate was related to another which several regions and the federal board had to talk and pray over. Surely, it was argued, a lot of loose edges and grey areas could be avoided if Mission England had a doctrinal basis which clearly stated what it did and did not believe.

It had to be admitted, however, that even evangelicals united in their determination to work together to proclaim the gospel of forgiveness and new life through the incarnate, crucified and risen Jesus, would be hard put to agree on a statement. Some would want more i's dotted and t's crossed than others. And people who might not accept the labels, but who wanted to be involved and to bring their non-Christian contacts, would be excluded altogether and so miss out on the spiritual benefits of coming under the sound of the gospel.

No-one on either team believed Christian belief was unimportant, nor did they wish to compromise. What they worked and prayed for was that the meetings and the structures would be channels of God's Spirit. And so they were.

Sight for strained eyes

Normally, people were not referred to nurture groups until they had gone forward. One man, however, had already reserved a place on one for his 65 year old mother. His faith was rewarded when she went forward one night.

One counsellor's faith came in for a jolt after she had talked to a disabled person who was unable to walk and had lost the use of an arm after a stroke nine years ago. She was a Christian, but wanted assurance that if she kept praying for healing God would answer her. The counsellor adopted a common approach and said that it was a good idea to keep praying but that 'she shouldn't feel God wasn't listening if she wasn't healed.'

A week later the disabled person phoned to say that she was walking and could use her arm and hand. 'We chatted for a long time about the power of the Lord.'

An 80 year old man, almost blind and partially deaf, went forward one night at Anfield. He had often asked Jesus into his life but nothing had happened. He said he was lonely.

His counsellor showed him a diagram which the man could just make out. On one side was a block representing God, and on the other a block representing the individual; between them was a gap, the sinfulness which separates God and man. Only Jesus' death on the cross could bridge the gap.

'Now I see!' exclaimed the blind man. 'I didn't realise that was why Jesus came.' His expression changed to one of complete joy. As he was leaving the ground he added, 'I know my body's jiggered, but I'll do what I can to serve him for the rest of my days.'

Two Christian Police Association members acting as stewards and security officers just could not believe their eyes one night. A couple of well known pickpockets had gone down into the counselling area during the invitation. Their police shadows kept a close watch on them, hoping to save any hapless enquirer or counsellor from losing their wallet or handbag. The pickpockets had not gone forward to get cash, however, but to be counselled.

It was the custom on the final day at most of the missions to thank the police for their security and traffic duty. This was done in Liverpool, and as elsewhere there was a spontaneous round of applause. One senior officer in the city later commented, 'The applause meant a great deal to my lads. Usually when they're handling crowd situations, they expect trouble. It took them time to realise all those thousands of people were truly friendly and well-behaved.

'The police hear a lot of the so-called silent majority who are supposed to be in sympathy with them, but they don't see much evidence of it. Now they've seen that majority surface and it has given them new heart.'

There was an added personal element in the mission for this particular officer, too. He took his daughter along and they went forward. David Alton, the MP, took his two friends forward one night. Speaking to the press later, he said, 'I took the opportunity as Dr Graham suggested to us all, to rededicate my life to Christ.'

And while this had been happening in Anfield, as it had at Ashton Gate, Roker Park, Carrow Road and Villa Park, and would at Portman Road Ipswich, some unsung and largely unreported things of a similar nature were happening outside the soccer grounds...

13

Highways and byways

Sunderland shopping centre is typical of many in England built or redeveloped during the 1960s and 1970s. The pedestrian precinct between the two rows of shops is no wider than an average single carriageway road; it always feels crowded but never crushed. Down the middle there are small trees in concrete tubs, and a few seats.

One day in June 1984, the cold wind of the past few days having abated and the temperature having risen a little closer to the norm for the time of year, 35 year old bearded evangelist Dave Glover leaned his easel and paint board against a waste bin and started to tell the shoppers about Billy Graham and the message he was proclaiming that week at Roker Park soccer ground.

In the crowd that paused to listen was a punk rocker; shaved and spiky hair, studded jacket. He did not like the message, and spat twice at Dave Glover to prove it. The other people standing there clearly felt that this was ungentlemanly conduct and told him so in that blunt manner typical of northern England.

'It was incredible,' Dave Glover said later. 'I thought he was going to get lynched!'

Dave Glover was one of the large team of British and American evangelists who took to the highways and byways while Billy Graham was in town to preach to those who would listen and to encourage them to go to the stadium meetings. In most cases the friendly reception of the Sunderland shoppers was repeated in other locations.

Down in Rugby, 25 miles east of Birmingham and within the catchment area for the Villa Park meetings, John Allan and his music group Extrax held an open air meeting in the town centre. In one and a half hours 40 people had signed up to join a bus to hear Billy Graham.

There were a few conversions, too, out on the streets. In Birmingham itself Rob Frost saw one person become a Christian on the first day of a series of open-air meetings. In Newcastle, black American rock singer Jimmy Mamou (who also sang during some of the stadium meetings) led some people to faith in Christ who were listening to him in the city's Eldon Square, a patch of grass close by the shopping centre.

Several regions extended their offices into the streets. In Birmingham there were Mission England stalls in the Bullring shopping centre and New Street railway station. Manned by members of Birmingham City Mission, they were issuing tickets for meetings, giving information about transport, selling books and of course talking to people about Christ.

In Bristol, a counselling trailer was parked in the yard of Wesley's historic chapel just off the shopping precinct. A handful of people called in for help, and one person became a Christian. In Chester, some distance from Liverpool but with huge support for the mission, a drop in centre was opened before and during the week of the Anfield meetings. In Liverpool itself, Mission England rented an empty shop opposite Anfield stadium for three months, where people could call in, have coffee, get tickets, and talk.

Open-air work can be rewarding. Students from Birmingham Bible Institute, and church members in Sunderland, who joined in open airs to talk personally to passers-by said that the experience had changed their whole attitude to evangelism; they realised just how willing people are to talk about Christian things. But the main purpose of the 'extension ministry', as it was called, was not to scatter the word quite so randomly. It is a hit and miss method, and the Mission England evangelists were looking for places where the ground had been better prepared.

Back to school

Schools provided some of them with golden opportunities. Head teachers were often willing to allow individuals or teams to take assemblies (short worship periods before morning lessons) or religious education classes. In the North West region Assistant Bishop of Liverpool, the Rt. Rev. Bill Flagg, who was also Mission England regional chairman, wrote to the schools and a large number responded positively with invitations for visits. In the South West, evangelist Korky Davey gave over 100 Christians some basic training in schools work so they could respond to the opportunities which were there for the taking.

Under British law, evangelism as such is not allowed in schools, but religious assemblies and religious education are compulsory. The evangelists were able to talk about Mission England, Billy Graham, and what they stood for, and tell youngsters where they could get buses to the stadium meetings. In classes they could of course answer questions on anything.

Ian Knox was one speaker, like many others, who found wherever he went that the teenage school children were asking 'genuine up-front questions'. 'What difference does being a Christian make?' 'How do you know God is in your life?' 'How do I know Jesus Christ?' It tallied with Billy Graham's own reflections on his ministry to students at Oxford and Cambridge Universities in 1980, and more recently at American universities including Harvard and Yale.

'I hardly ever get questions about science and the Bible,' he said on several occasions. 'Young people today are more interested in knowing what life is all about.'

It also revealed that sometimes people are much nearer

commitment to Christ than their Christian friends imagine. One schoolgirl said she could not give her life to Christ because she could not understand what heaven was all about. Ian Knox told her that questions of that kind need not be a barrier to actually trusting Jesus here and now, and this she found helpful. Her Christian friends had been spending too long trying to answer the question and making Christianity seem complicated in the process.

Tough assignments

There was a mixed bag of engagements in factories and other institutions. Among the more unusual places where Mission England evangelists could speak were a poultry farm, a maternity hospital, and two breweries. Jimmy Mamou and British evangelist Roy Crowne were allowed into the canteen at Ford's car factory at Ellesmere Port on Merseyside. They talked to the men personally and then had five minutes to speak publicly about the Billy Graham meetings in nearby Liverpool. Roy Crowne also did a walkabout in Avonmouth docks near Bristol. The short, stocky preacher was faced by a huge burly man none too sympathetic to his message; 'It was the nearest I have ever been to backing down,' he said.

One disappointment on the industrial front was a policy decision made by chaplains to factories and shipyards in the North East not to allow in any Mission England team members; extension task group chairman John Hood received a letter from the Northumbrian Industrial Mission asking for no approaches to be made to individual firms. In the same region, the managing director of a large retail company was initially sympathetic to the idea of a meeting in the staff canteen. But after he consulted the company's chaplain, the request was turned down.

But a quite different picture emerged from what are often regarded as the hardest of all situations for evangelism: the armed services, the police, and prisons. The Royal Engineers at Stratford-on-Avon had reportedly 'eaten alive' local clergy who the chaplain had invited in. Roy Crowne was given half an hour for his lecture; he stayed for an additional hour answering perfectly serious and searching questions. Gordon Bridger went to speak at a military college; it was a holiday and only a dozen people came to the meeting. But the wife of a senior officer got up and said she wanted to become a Christian.

Up in the North East, two Christians in a police training centre got their Commandant's permission to hold a Mission England meeting. They expected 20 people to come to it, but 100 turned up, including senior officers. The speaker had been allocated 15 minutes; the meeting continued spontaneously for two hours.

In the prisons, Americans Ralph Bell, Howard Jones and Jimmy Mamou had a special and at times spectacular ministry. A young people's detention centre in Rugby had specifically requested an English evangelist; none was available, but Jimmy Mamou was. And where an American was thought to be unsuitable, over a dozen young men gave their lives to Christ.

There were commitments to Christ in every prison which evangelists visited; Winson Green, Strangeways, and Walton among them. To the surprise expressed at the results, one evangelist replied, 'What do you expect? We're not preaching to the converted.' And therein lies the rub.

A high proportion of extension meetings were organised by churches which gave their midweek or special meetings to Mission England, and by Christian Unions in offices, hospitals and colleges. They were almost without exception disappointing. The Christians had not been able to bring their non-Christian friends along. At the headquarters of the National Girobank in Liverpool, for example, only four people, all Christians, turned up for an evangelistic meeting. In Newmarket, in East Anglia, one person turned up at a special Christian Union meeting.

There were some notable exceptions. At Sandwell Hospital near Birmingham the Christians brought their colleagues. Out of an attendance of 40, nine responded to the invitation to become Christians. And in Leicester, at a lunchtime businessman's meeting at Holy Trinity Church, Ian Knox asked people who wished to become Christians to give their names in at the end. The girl who was writing them down took the names of four of her office colleagues, among others.

The extension work was not helped by organisational problems. It had tended to be the Cinderella activity, and local areas were slow to catch on to the idea; they were more concerned with filling buses to the stadium meetings. British and American evangelists were organised by different people, and this sometimes led to confusion. On the British side, it was decided to handle all bookings centrally so that there would be a minimum number of incidents where evangelists were given opportunities which did not suit their gifts. But there was only one person to handle the administration; meetings were sometimes arranged at the last minute; and evangelists' availability was not always clear or consistent until close to the time.

But if more might have been made of extension ministry, it did at least take the Christian message into places others might not have reached. George Hamilton IV never quite got over the fact that for the first time in his country and western life he sang in a barn. About 1000 people sat on straw bales in Blandford St Mary, Dorset to hear him, along with a local group Lovelight and evangelist Don Summers – and 100 people came forward at the end. Don Summers also had the experience of preaching at a church in Barnstaple, Devon, the day after a party had been at a stadium meeting; he gave an invitation for public declaration of faith and 50 responded, most of whom had been on the verge of getting out of their seats at Ashton Gate, Bristol.

Broadcasting history

Although not within the orbit of extension ministry organisers, but certainly within the definition of the work, were some history-making broadcasts of stadium meetings.

In Sunderland, an hour of the Sunday evening meeting was broadcast live to Britain on BBC Radio 4 and also carried by the BBC World Service, which is beamed around the earth and is a lifeline for expatriots and for nationals who do not always receive reliable news and current affairs information from their local networks. It was the first such broadcast ever carried on the World Service, and although the potential listening audience of 60 million quoted at the time was probably higher than actually tuned in, the numbers must still have been unimaginably huge.

In several regions local radio stations carried a live meeting, and the hospital radio system, which uses telephone landlines to give soccer commentaries to patients, also broadcast meetings at each venue. In Birmingham, however, it took on a new dimension. First, the local hospital radio station offered the sound to similar organisations anywhere in Britian. It was taken up by several, from Burnley in Lancashire to Tunbridge Wells in Kent.

Then someone realised that with a little help from British Telecom, it would be technically possible for private telephone subscribers to tap in to the sound too. The national telephone system duly laid on 220 lines, all of which were engaged for most of the eight meetings. One of the listeners was Billy Graham's wife Ruth, a few days before she finally flew to England to join her husband.

Some 13 hours of coverage was given to Mission meetings on radio and TV. Much of it was in small news clips in regional magazine programmes, but there were larger features too. Among the more significant was a series of interviews with Billy Graham by Colin Morris, head of BBC Religious Broadcasting. Each interview, aired in August, looked at one of the four horsemen in the biblical book of Revelation, the subject of Billy Graham's recently published book. It turned into a serious, although wide-ranging, discussion about the issues which face the world, and the Christian response to them. To round off the series, BBC 2 broadcast at peak time a 90 minute recording of the Wednesday night meeting at Villa Park, Birmingham.

It was the second mission meeting to be televised. The day after the Sunderland mission closed, the Independent TV network broadcast a recording of the Wednesday meeting at Roker Park – where thankfully the weather had by then improved – as the main Sunday morning TV service.

A special office was set up in Sheffield to handle the mail from these broadcasts; viewers and listeners were invited to write in for counselling literature. Some 10,000 people did, with probably about three per cent indicating that they had become Christians through the broadcasts. Over 7,000 of those letters came from the BBC telecast which was seen by an estimated 1.8 million people; BBC TV normally receives only 2000 letters a week on editorial matters.

'I watched the programme on TV last night,' wrote a clergyman from the Midlands. 'It seemed that what Dr Graham was saying was addressed directly to me. I want to rededicate my life to Christ, but I need to talk to someone. Will you help me?'

An 87 year old from the North West wrote saying he would never forget the broadcast. 'I have been a committed Christian from early boyhood but unfortunately with many lapses. But on Friday night I again in the privacy of my heart gave myself again to Jesus. I feel just wonderful after it.'

It all added to the excitement, wonder and magnitude of the outreach in the summer of 1984. And at Ipswich, the last of the six missions, a rather bewildered 15 year old boy stepped into the history books as Mission England reached another milestone...

Note: Among other evangelists sharing in extension ministry were Roy Gustafson of the BGEA and some 20 British people including Rob Frost, Peter Green, Gordon Bridger and Derek Cook.

14

Clocking up a million

Portman Road, Ipswich, 24–28 July

It was Friday 27 July at Portman Road football ground, Ipswich. The millionth person to come through the turnstiles to hear Billy Graham during his summer tour in England was about to arrive. The fact itself was probably irrelevant so far as God's economy goes, but to human beings caught up in the unexpected thrill of seeing full grounds and high responses, it was a little milestone they did not want to ignore. Besides, it was fun, good and wholesome to boot, like a birthday.

The stadium staff kept a tally of the people entering Portman Road; when the figure was within 100 of the number required to bring the cumulative attendance to one million, BGEA London Director Maurice Rowlandson went into action. Standing at the main entrance, he turned his back on the streaming crowd so that he would not be influenced by a face, and began the countdown as people passed him. Nervous team members prayed that the person upon whose shoulder Maurice Rowlandson's hand fell would be young and male. (Young and female on a newspaper front page might look embarrassingly similar to the sales hype which spreads girls across car bonnets; old and either sex would be untypical of the high percentage of young people who came to hear Billy Graham.) The press men didn't care who it was so long as he or she was local.

At 7.20 p.m. Maurice Rowlandson sprang, and some prayers were answered. Alan Paget, looking a little older than his 15 years, was escorted onto the turf to meet Billy Graham. The evangelist presented him with a book and a Mission England sweatshirt, and the electronic scoreboard announced the magic number to the crowd. The press photographers clicked their shutters and said their editors probably wouldn't mind; Alan Paget had come with a group from Honor Oak Baptist Church, East Dulwich, in south London, way beyond the usual catchment area for the Ipswich mission and the circulation area for the local papers.

But then that had been the story all through the summer; coaches from Scotland went to Sunderland, one was ferried across from Ireland to Holyhead in North Wales and then driven on to Liverpool. Birmingham had a party from the Scandinavian Faroes Islands, and Ipswich welcomed a German delegation. Billy Graham was worth travelling to.

Indeed, people from a much wider area than usual were expected at Ipswich, although not until the following day, the last meeting in the Mission England series.

Last thoughts

The British and BGEA leadership had been long vexed over the problem of a finale to the stadium phase of Mission England. At first they had considered a large London gathering, but that would have interfered with the work of Mission to London. Luis Palau, of Argentinian origin but now a naturalised American, had booked Loftus Road, the West London home of soccer club Queens Park Rangers, for four weeks of meetings in June 1984 to follow up his series of area missions around greater London in the autumn of 1983; the four weeks was later extended to six going into July.

The evangelists were good friends; they visited each others' missions and exchanged public greetings. Luis Palau went to Norwich on his free night, and Billy Graham went to London during the two week interval between Norwich and Birmingham. The organisers of both missions had kept each other abreast of their plans, meeting together from time to time and exchanging committee meeting minutes. They held a joint day of prayer early in 1984. Each referred their own enquirers to the others' nurture groups, too, if they lived in that region. They were not rivals, and they decided that the cause of the gospel would be best served if they each kept to their own designated areas.

Another possibility for a national finale was Sheffield, centre of the famous steel and cutlery trade, and close to large Yorkshire industrial towns. In August 1982 Christian leaders in the city had indicated their interest in a Billy Graham mission, and by December that year the BGEA were in favour of it in principle, if it could be fitted into the schedule.

All kinds of permutations were attempted. Linking the North West with Yorkshire and having the mission split between venues in Sheffield and Liverpool or Manchester was one suggestion, but that would have done neither region justice. Cutting a day or two from other missions would have helped, but it would have been hardly fair. And although a fortnight's break in the middle of Mission England gave the appearance of spare time, it was part of the contract that Billy Graham would be kept completely free during it.

The solution would have been relatively easy if the original five regions of Mission England had not evolved, amoeba-like, into six, while Billy Graham's time block remained the same. The East Anglian pressure for a mission came originally from Norwich in the north of the region, via Bishop Maurice Wood. Victor Jack, a free church evangelist who ran Sizewell Hall, a Christian conference and camping centre was closely in touch with the plans, and along with others from the south of the region argued strongly that people from the Ipswich area would not travel in large numbers to Norwich, 40 miles to the north. That made it unlikely that the thinly populated region could maintain an eight day mission, and a vital regional centre would not be serviced properly by the mission.

The decision to split East Anglia into two regions with four days mission in each was made at an early stage of the planning. The arguments were convincing and no-one on the English and American teams ultimately had any reason for doubting the decision. But even though the number of actual days' mission remained the same, the time involved in getting the team in place in East Anglia was doubled, because the exercise had to be done twice.

One final possibility remained. If Ipswich could follow straight on from Norwich in the same week there could be a three day event in Sheffield. It would have been a practical nightmare for the team, but at least the two places were not very far apart. However, the Anglicans in the Ipswich Diocese already had plans for a large celebration of the Diocese's seventieth anniversary, with the Archbishop of Canterbury present, very close to the proposed new dates.

The Bishop of St Edmundsbury and Ipswich, the Rt. Rev. John Wayne, who encouraged clergy to support Mission England, was unable to change the dates of the celebration. If the Billy Graham mission was close to it, he feared that the clergy and people would have their energies and loyalties split. So by April 1983, the dates for all the regional missions were confirmed as they had been set originally.

That left two problems: Sheffield was disappointed and there was still no special concluding meeting. The latter was solved in early June, when Billy Graham asked for an extra day at Ipswich. It was the only venue on the original schedule which did not have a Saturday meeting; its four days were Tuesday to Friday. By altering his flight plans to Korea in July, Billy Graham could stay on for an extra day. And people around London and in the Midlands would have the chance to travel a not unreasonable distance at a weekend to swell the audience.

As for Sheffield, after an agonising period of uncertainty, it came out on top. After the conclusion of the Ipswich mission Billy Graham announced a decision which had been troubling him, like the Russian invitation, all summer. He would accept the invitation to lead a full eight day mission in Sheffield in 1985.

It had been a struggle; like others in Mission England it

turned out to be creative. God does not always make his ways and plans as clear as the noonday sun. Faith and patience are sometimes tested, but as a result confidence and conviction are increased and service and sacrifice are inspired.

The ending, as far as Ipswich was concerned, did not look at first as if it was going to be entirely happy. The local authority and the police were very anxious about the extra traffic congestion the meeting would cause in a town which always had a huge influx of shoppers on Saturday afternoon. Then when the organisers started to think about chartering special trains from different parts of the country, they discovered that on Saturday 28 July 1984 British Rail would have no stock to spare; it was the peak summer holiday travelling day. Buses, too, were hard to find. By changing the time of the meeting from 3.30 p.m. to 6.00 p.m., they helped the police, and got a special train from London.

It was not the vast throng which had invaded Wembley in 1966 that came to Ipswich that day; 18,504 people basked in warm evening sunshine at Portman Road. But that was perhaps appropriate. Mission England was essentially national, but it was especially regional. Each venue had already said its farewells and had expressed its thanks to God and to the team. The last day was for East Anglia as much as it was for England.

The people who came heard Billy Graham describe that spiritual vacuum and hunger he had often alluded to in the previous three months. He spoke of a sense of loneliness and a lack of identity; of a search for purpose, meaning and hope; of a concern about seemingly insoluble social needs, and the impossible moral decisions which have to be made; of a sense of guilt, a shallow lifestyle and an awareness of spiritual reality which the cults were ready to exploit.

Mike was someone aware of that spiritual hunger. He listened to the Wednesday night meeting as it was broadcast on local radio, and he wanted to become a Christian. A CB radio enthusiast, he called up another CB operator and told him his need.

'My neighbour is a Christian,' said the man. 'I'll let you

talk with him.'

The neighbour was called in, and he led Mike to Christ over the radio. The next night they went together to Portman Road.

Ipswich, in fact, had its share of unusual stories. Nadine Peakall's husband asked her what she wanted for her birthday. She asked for a bus to take people to the Portman Road meetings to hear Billy Graham. He agreed, and all but one seat was filled.

Then there were the newlyweds who gave up their honeymoon to help at the stadium; their task was to clean the temporary toilets.

And there was Gordon, who worked in the follow-up room, processing the cards counsellors filled in while talking to enquirers. He reported for duty as usual one night after the meeting, and he was given a pile of cards to sort. The top one was that of Iris, his wife, for whom he had prayed for many years.

Night owls

When Iris had gone forward, she first had to squeeze her way past other people sitting in her row; but people all around her were moving, so she did not feel too conspicuous. Then she walked down the exit stairs to ground level, and under the stand. There was a wooden staircase with a handrail to cross the perimeter wall before she finally stood on the grass. She followed the other people towards the blue-draped platform which at Ipswich was closer to the centre of the playing area than at other missions; there was not quite so far to walk.

Feeling perhaps nervous, or excited, or just a little self-conscious, Iris stood behind a group of other people, and quickly the space around her filled up with others. Some were wearing badges.

After the final prayer, a woman with a counsellor's badge came up to Iris and introduced herself. She showed Iris a card with five possible responses which she might have made printed on it: 'Receive Christ for the first time;' 'Don't have assurance that my sins are forgiven;' 'I have received Jesus but I am seeking his forgiveness;' 'I have received Jesus but I am demonstrating my faith;' 'I have a special need I would like to discuss with someone.'

Iris ticked the one which applied to her. The counsellor talked with her about her decision, and showed her the literature which she would take home. Then the counsellor filled in a card with Iris's name, address, age, occupation, and details of her church connections, before they prayed together and parted.

As Iris made her way home, the counsellor gave the card to a collector on the pitch. He took it to the follow-up room, where Gordon was waiting, having already reported for duty.

The follow-up room at Ipswich was the soccer club's gymnasium. (In Liverpool it had been the trophy room, lined with cups, plates and medals won over the years.) It had required some building works, as had the room in Birmingham; a new fire escape was erected to make the gymnasium safe for 300 people to work in.

Those people who worked through the night, sometimes until 4.00 a.m., were the unsung heroes of Mission England in every venue. They were a mixed bunch; in Bristol a statistics Ph.D was sorting cards and a medical doctor made the tea. In Birmingham a 70 year old lady who had fallen down and had five stitches in her gashed head during the day turned up for work at 9.30 that evening as usual. No region was ever short of volunteers; in Ipswich and Birmingham the queue often lingered until 1.00 a.m. in case a vacancy should occur. Without that painstaking work many enquirers would not have been linked with nurture groups for some time.

In days of yore, it sometimes took weeks for a minister to be notified of an enquirer's decision, and there was no guarantee he would follow them up quickly. But after years of experience the BGEA had got the system down to a fine art. During Mission England it was for some enquirers only a matter of hours before a nurture group leader called; most would expect to be contacted within a few days.

It was at this point that some of the painstaking preparatory work which had not met with enthusiasm in the regional offices slipped into place like a mysterious piece in a jigsaw puzzle which hitherto had defied recognition.

Each region had been asked to produce a list of churches, which were held on computer at the national office in Harrow. The follow-up room in each region was sent twenty copies of each of four print-outs: one listing churches by the minister's name, one by postal town, one by post code, and one by denomination. The post code had been hard to discover, as few churches use a postal address, but it was to prove essential in linking enquirers to nurture groups in cases where the follow-up team were unfamiliar with the district or town. There was also a complete set of British post codes, for enquirers' cards which did not have them filled in.

Iris's card was emptied, along with many others, onto a table marked 'statistics'. The follow-up room was filled with long rows of uncovered trestle tables, each section clearly marked with a red and white sign to indicate what function took place at it. Here, the cards were counted and analysed according to age, sex and response. The figures for the evening were usually completed by midnight.

Then Iris's card went to 'sorting', depending upon what else needed doing to it, before passing to one of 120 people who worked in the 'research' section. Their task was to locate the appropriate nurture group and complete any information missing from the card.

That was the first half of the process; the next was to ensure that Iris received a letter from Billy Graham to encourage her to press on with her new-found faith, and that a suitable nurture group leader was notified of Iris's commitment and could contact her quickly. After a check to see all the information was filled in, typists would prepare envelopes to Iris and the nurture group leader, and complete a standard letter with Iris's details to be sent to the group leader.

After another check, envelopes were stuffed, franked, and ultimately taken for posting through the still and silent streets which even insomniacs had by that time deserted for their beds. Letters to the same postal town or city sometimes arrived later that day, enabling the keenest of nurture group leaders to call less than 24 hours after the enquirer had gone forward.

Mission England Director of Training Eddie Gibbs reckons that mistakes were made in up to 10 per cent of cases, often because the information on the card was incomplete when it came in; counsellors were not always meticulous. In many cases, however, churches swapped enquirers who would fit better somewhere else.

The difficult cases, in which there was no obvious nurture group, were tackled by a designation committee the following morning. They selected three churches of different denominations in the area if the enquirer had no preference, one or two if they did. In the afternoon a team of clergy would make the final choice, and their work was monitored for early warning signs of denominational bias.

The follow-up room was equipped with tables, chairs and 40 typewriters bought for the purpose before Bristol and sold after Ipswich. (The first night in Bristol typists were sitting on hassocks on top of ordinary chairs. This proved so uncomfortable that the next day Mission England bought 40 proper typists' chairs.)

The equipment was transported from place to place (along with all the rest of the stadium requirements, including those thin flat plastic cushions for the concrete terraces) in two large trucks belonging to David Vardy, stadium chairman in the North East. He believed in getting all the publicity for Mission England he could, so he painted the sides of the trucks with the Mission England-Billy Graham logo together with the dates and venues of all the meetings.

In charge of transportation was Dennis Barden, a former civil servant who lived near Gavin Reid in Surrey. Ipswich presented him with his biggest headache of the tour.

The Liverpool mission ended on Saturday night; Ipswich on the opposite side of England with no cross-country motorway for part of the run, opened on Tuesday night. He had a couple of days instead of the normal five, and of course

everyone except the follow-up team wanted *their* equipment
in Ipswich before even Liverpool had finished; the follow up
team wanted theirs kept in Liverpool until the day Ipswich
began. It was all right on the night, even though Dennis
Barden and helpers were unloading cushions as the crowds
came through the turnstiles.

Slow growth

All that was in the future for Victor Jack as he took on the
chairmanship of East Anglia (South). Like the northern half
the region is largely rural, although Colchester and Chelms-
ford provide additional clusters of urban population besides
Ipswich. Lakenheath nearby has the largest garrison of US
servicemen in Europe, and they swelled the audience by
between 800 and 1100 each night.

Victor Jack already knew many church leaders in the
region, but he decided that the only way to arouse support for
the mission was to meet people face to face. He kept a tally on
the meetings he spoke at; 12,500 people heard him speak
specifically about Mission England.

As in the North, it took some time for enthusiasm to grow.
The regional committee set its target attendance at 75,000;
they in fact had more than that after the four nights they had
originally planned for, and the fifth meeting brought the total
to over 90,000.

Among them were 2,000 'special guests' – local political,
community, commercial and industrial leaders – who had
'silver delegation' seats in the Directors' Box. Ipswich had
made them a special concern, and several went forward.
They mingled with almost 7500 enquirers, over eight per
cent of the attendance, a proportion almost identical to that
with which Mission England had begun in Bristol eleven
weeks earlier.

Johnny Lenning had been in England with the BGEA
team for that period, working as the sound recordist and
putting *Hour of Decision* radio programmes together. In
Ipswich he had a letter from his daughter. She had planted a

vegetable garden after he left America; she reported that she had already eaten most of the produce.

By then in England the oilseed rape had obediently gone to seed, and sprays of elder flower had taken over from hawthorn as the white garnish on the hedgerows. The standing corn glowed golden in the summer sun, ripe for the harvest which had just begun on some Suffolk farms.

Victor Jack, stripped to the waist, was sweeping the empty terraces at Portman Road. The harsh clinking of scaffold poles and joints being dismantled echoed round the ground. In the little cabin in the yard which served as the Mission England regional office, vibrating from the machinery in the tobacco factory a few yards away, administrator John Sherman began winding up the paperwork.

It was all over. The Billy Graham phase of Mission England was complete. And yet it was also destined to continue. Responsible for the apparent paradox was Mission England vice chairman, David Rennie, and his electronic box of tricks...

15

Sight and sound

In 1967, the Billy Graham team pioneered a huge technical operation in Britain. The meetings at Earl's Court, London, were televised and live signals sent via telephone landline to 26 centres throughout the country. The image was projected onto large screens in theatres, town halls and even an old bus garage. The 'All Britain TV Crusade' drew half a million people to the relay centres and 200,000 to Earl's Court itself.

Masterminding the operation was electronics expert David Rennie. It was so successful that German Christians asked him to oversee the TV relay of the Billy Graham mission in Dortmund in 1970; it went to 36 venues in eleven European countries and was translated into eight languages. His services were required again in 1974 at the huge Eurofest conference. He called his task 'unscrambling Babel'; he had to make simultaneous translation into eight languages possible through loudspeakers, not earphones, in the same hall, yet so that each group could hear only its own language.

In 1978 he spent six months in Scandinavia supervising the TV relays for a Graham mission. It was something of a turning point for him. He had tried for three years to set up a company specialising in renting out electronics equipment, but had not succeeded. On Good Friday 1978 he laid his plans aside and went to Scandinavia. Six months later he picked up the files again, and his new company was off the ground in a matter of weeks.

When the plans for Billy Graham's 1984 English missions were first laid, people all over Britain began asking if TV relays could be fed to their localities. They could not. The cost of renting landlines had increased astronomically, and the project was not economically viable.

But David Rennie had other ideas. The video boom had begun to break in Britain, which already had one of the world's highest concentrations of home video recorders per head of population. Video was more flexible than landline relay. It could be used in a home, in a small church or hall with several domestic TVs as monitors, and in bigger venues using large screen projection. Recorders and projection equipment were relatively cheap to hire, and bulk duplication of tapes would help to reduce production costs and spread the capital cost of the actual recording.

Furthermore, there were companies which could guarantee fast overnight duplication of tapes, and the Datapost system guaranteed next day delivery of packets anywhere in the UK. Videos of, say, Tuesday's meeting could be seen anywhere in Britain on Wednesday. The video mission was born.

As with other Mission England projects, it was some time before the idea took its final shape. Extensive market research was needed before David Rennie could know which missions it would be best to record in order to meet the demand – if, indeed, the demand existed. A large number of missions would be required to make the venture self-financing, and so commitment rather than passing interest was required from potential purchasers. But even though the tapes would cost £250 for a set of four, David Rennie and Mission England staff were insisting that they could only be sold to people who organised and ran a proper mini-mission with adequate counsellor training and as many of the other Mission England features as possible. They had no desire to foster pockets of home video entertainment.

At a fairly late stage it was decided to abandon the next-day delivery; Tuesday's tapes would be available instead on

Thursday. It was a wise decision. Technical hitches on one occasion in Bristol delayed the completion of the editing until 3.00 a.m. But on normal evenings, the extra time allowed for more quality control and more efficient editing by a team who could sleep before working on it the next morning.

The market research pointed to Bristol and Birmingham as being the most suitable missions to record. But that was not without its problems, too, as the Rev. James Howarth and his friends discovered in Bridlington, a town on the East Yorkshire coast.

Night vision

The Bridlington video mission caught the imagination if for no other reason than that the organisers decided to hold it in a night club. A popular restaurant in the town, which became a night club in the late evening, provided a setting in which non-Christians might feel more comfortable than in a church. It had a large room suitable for over 200 people, and the management proved very co-operative.

James Howarth, the local Mission England convener, booked it for May, and the videos from Bristol. To have held the mission any later would have clashed with the holiday season; visitors to the seaside town would come, but local residents would be less able to.

Then the recording of the Bristol meetings was cancelled. Billy Graham was understandably uneasy at the prospect of preaching to camera before he had really got the feel of a country he had not visited extensively for some years. Preaching to both a large stadium and also to the unblinking eye of a camera is never easy at the best of times.

James Howarth was stunned. He and his fellow organisers had been absolutely convinced that May was God's time for their mission. They decided to pray that Billy Graham would change his mind.

One day, when James Howarth's telephone rang, Susan Pannell, BGEA team member who was helping David Rennie administer the video project, was on the line.

'Are you still interested in a May video mission?' she asked. 'Mr Graham's changed his mind and given the go-ahead to record Bristol.'

Four churches had worked together to organise the Bridlington mission. About 1,000 people attended the four meetings, requiring an overflow in a church down the road; the TV cable was draped along the balconies of shops between restaurant and church. But only 15 people went forward. Bridlington had discovered what other video missions were also finding out.

It was clearly not easy for people to go forward, especially in a relatively small place, to stand in front of an impersonal TV screen. The unnaturalness of Orwell's fictional giant screens dictating movement in home and workplace had a basis in fact. When a live person stood at the front and invited members of the audience to go forward, more tended to respond; there was someone to go to who would tell them what to do next.

Some people also said the prayer of commitment audibly in their seats; James Howarth reported a 'murmur of prayer' each night. Some asked for literature after the meeting, although not for counselling as such.

The video missions often suffered through lack of adequate preparation time. Prayer triplets and Operation Andrew rarely took root. Visitation was hardly attempted on any scale. If nothing else, the response at the video missions underlined the absolute necessity for prayer and friendship evangelism to precede any form of centralised outreach.

None of the mission organisers thought that their video outreach was a waste of time, however. As in the stadium missions, Christians benefitted from working together and being trained for evangelism. And reports filtered back indicating that a number of people who had seen the videos were becoming Christians in the weeks afterwards. A chaplain in the British armed forces in Germany said that three conversions after the mission more than made up for his disappointment that no-one had come forward at the showings. The Mission England national office at Harrow received a letter from a 63 year old lady saying that she wished she had gone forward and could she please have the literature.

Steve was in his mid 20s, unemployed, and he had no church connections. Wandering aimlessly through the Essex town in which he lived, he saw the posters advertising the video mission. They made him decide that he ought to have a Bible. He bought one, and began to read it. Without any human prompting or invitation, he went to the video meeting. He was the first to step forward to the front.

An estimated 200,000 people attended the 208 videos held up to the end of July 1984, with around 6,000 people having sought counsel. Sheffield alone had eleven missions scattered through the city, giving organisers a dry run for the full-scale stadium mission planned for 1985.

And the tapes were made available after the stadium phase so that video missions could continue elsewhere.

Sound faith

David Rennie also took responsibility for the technical arrangements at the stadium meetings – sound, lights and camera placements. When things went wrong, he had to supervise the troubleshooting.

In Liverpool, for example, a problem with the electricity supply caused a hum on the sound system which made life impossible for the American TV crew recording the meetings. When all other efforts to eradicate it failed, he located a heavy industrial generator to provide power for the TV crew.

And it was he who approved the contract for the stadium sound being given to a 29 year old Englishman, Mike Spratt, who had his own story of faith to tell.

The sound system at the meetings was such that most people could hear speakers and soloists as clearly as if they were in the same room. Every stadium had its dead areas, corners where sound did not penetrate so freely, but the vast majority of listeners had no difficulty in hearing every word. Usually the main loud speakers were mounted on two scissor hoists standing on the turf, which could be raised or lowered according to the height of the stands round the ground. Only in Liverpool, where the heavy equipment could not be placed on the grass but had to be slung from the roofs of the stands, were there any real problems, and these affected mostly those people who sat at the front directly below the loudspeakers.

Mike Spratt's small company, Wigwam Acoustics, was based in the small Lancashire town of Heywood. He began his sound engineering work with a local gospel rock group, through whom he became a Christian. His first venture into large scale amplification happened when he went to hear the late David Watson at Manchester; the sound was so bad that Mike Spratt could hardly hear a word, and he offered to take over the sound. Today his firm provides sound equipment for a number of small and large Christian events, and also works for television companies.

Getting the Mission England contract happened only after Mike Spratt had taken a huge step of faith. Not knowing that there would be a need for high powered sound in soccer stadiums, he still felt impelled to buy the expensive equipment when he had an opportunity to do so. When Mission England approached him some time later, exactly the right equipment was waiting in his workshop.

That was typical of the Mission England story. It was an adventure of faith backed by careful and prayerful preparation. But what would happen after Billy Graham's visit? Mission England had been conceived as a three year, not a three month, programme.

Early in September 1984, David Vardy invited 20 men and women to his home in a village with the unlikely-sounding name of Hetton-le-Hole to discuss the issue as it related to the North East region. Outside in the garden, the roses were fading and the first leaves of autumn were falling to the lawn. Was it to be thanks for the memory and back to the winter of our churches' discontent? Or would there be some further splash of spiritual life and colour, like the dahlias bursting into bloom at the bottom of the Vardys' autumnal garden?...

16

The mission goes on

'Frankly,' says one North East task group leader, 'we should have set up new churches for young people because the existing ones can't cope with them.'

He is discussing the next stage of Mission England with 19 other task group and area leaders in David Vardy's house at Hetton-le-Hole near Sunderland. It is a suggestion which neither Mission England nor the BGEA could contemplate; their expressed intention has been to work with the churches, not against them or even in spite of them. But it raises a pressing issue: what will happen to the 96,982 enquirers who came forward at the 41 stadium meetings?

Clearly many had become well integrated into churches during the summer. 'Those who made a commitment are now not just in nurture groups but actually participating in church life,' wrote a Pentecostal minister from South Wales. From Berkshire, on the fringe of the Bristol catchment area, came the story of 14 teenagers belonging to a Christian youth group who went forward at Ashton Gate. 'The transformation this brought to our weekly meetings was simply wonderful,' wrote their leader. 'There has been an openness and eagerness to discuss spiritual things I had never known in four years of leading the group.'

And from Sunderland itself came the story of a young man who became a Christian at Roker Park. 'When I was asked to attend church,' he said, 'I went along without enthusiasm as church had always seemed a very boring place to me. It turned out to be the best thing I've ever done as the service was full of life and happiness. It really is wonderful to be a Christian!'

At each mission a considerable number of children went forward. Did they understand what they were doing? Sylvia was a mother who watched with surprise as her youngsters went forward; she felt no desire to join them.

'The children came home with their booklets and puzzles to do. They read a passage from St Luke each day and asked me questions on it. I answered as best I could but I had to read the passage first. After a few days I knew I was going to be questioned so I started to read the passage before they did.

'Life isn't quite the same now; we have a new way of looking at things, of overcoming our problem, knowing there is someone who *does* care about us. I didn't find Jesus at Bristol, my children did. He came home with them and found me here! And now I pray, "Jesus, please stay. Life is so much better since you came."'

Brenda Huddleston was a children's counsellor in Norwich and a task group leader. She said, 'The letters I've since received from the children really show that the Holy Spirit is working in their lives.' From another region came the story of an eight year old who had brought several friends along to the meetings and encouraged them to become Christians; she had given her own life to Christ when she was four. 'Who said child conversions don't stick?' asked a counsellor.

Not for a moment, however, could it be expected or imagined that everyone, child or adult, who went forward would stick immediately in churches or nurture groups. David Spriggs, a Baptist minister in Coventry and a Midlands region task group leader, said that 'a large proportion of those indicated as first time commitments which his church received 'were not really commitments but enquirers.'

Another minister, from Cheshire in the North West, concurred; 'Many of the decisions were purely cries for help and people do not want to be just shoved into a nurture group but need practical help and encouragement to know the Lord in reality working in their lives.'

That does not necessarily imply failure on the part of the mission or the nurture group. To take some tangible step forward to seek help for a felt need is the only way to find it, even if the solution does not come so quickly to one person as it does to another. The fact that people have complex human needs as well as spiritual needs throws great responsibility on those involved in follow-up to exercise patient, persistent and practical pastoral care for as long as it is accepted.

A further factor in the mixed longer-term results of any mission is found in Jesus' parable of the sower. He foretold that some people would indeed hear and respond but that they would soon fall away. In the providence of God, however, others do not. So, after a mission some stick and grow; some stumble, lie dormant for a while and perhaps get up again; others slide and never recover. That is a fact of life, not a criticism of evangelistic methods. If it happened to Jesus, it is more likely to happen to his followers. Billy Graham often referred to the parable, stressing that only God knew what was going on in a person's life.

The reason it sometimes becomes an issue with large scale evangelistic meetings is that they are among the few occasions in church life when people are given an opportunity to make a public response to the gospel. If no response is asked for, there is no possibility that people will fall away; there is also, of course, less likelihood that they will commit themselves to Christ. The risk of losing some has to be balanced against the benefit of leading others into the kingdom.

Nurture of new Christians had always been one of the aims of the third year of Mission England. The regions differed in their approach. The South West and the Midlands published new study courses so nurture groups could continue to meet and learn together.

The North East, as they talk together in Hetton-le-Hole, decide only to publicise existing material in their bulletins to churches in the region; they do not feel called to add to it. But they have a more difficult task to face.

Facing the future

One word bounces around the walls from person to person; it becomes almost a catchword, a slogan, a potential cliche; it has been echoed in other regions, too: 'credibility'.

'Mission England has credibility in peoples' eyes,' one person says. 'They've seen it's well organised.' (Pause as laughter ripples round the room, good humoured laughter springing from relief and satisfaction that the major slog is ended, the minor blunders are past, and many people are saved.) 'There's a lot of good will around. People's theological suspicions have been to an extent overcome, and barriers between churches have been broken down. There's been co-operation between fellowships which once would have hardly spoken to each other. Now they want to continue to work together.'

The success of the Billy Graham mission has hinged largely on the evangelist's personal ability to motivate and hold together Christians on the basis of their common faith in the crucified and risen Christ and their shared concern to bring others into a personal experience of Christ. It is possible that Mission England can continue that role, the North East leaders decide. But how?

In the short term the question is easily answered. A series of meetings, 'PS to Roker', are planned to take place around the region, with an evangelistic thrust and an element of thanksgiving. Other regions too have put similar plans together. The main thrust of Mission England Year 3 is for further evangelism at a local level.

National Director Gavin Reid had often expressed a concern for one category of people who rarely feature in strategies and never end up in statistics. In a letter to regional chairmen as far back as November 1983 he wrote, 'In ten years of participating in local church evangelism and in trying to think about evangelism in general I would say that our biggest mistake has always been the lack of a strategy following evangelistic missions concerning those who are "almost persuaded".' In year three, he said, he could see many new possibilities through supper evenings, church evangelistic services, business lunches and so on.

Mission England had provided many Christians in local churches with training, enthusiasm and confidence to do things they had never dreamed possible: to knock on strangers' doors, to counsel enquirers, to use their organising skills for the church and so feel less like pew fodder and more like members of some great interdependant team.

John Hood, from the North East, said Mission England had taught his church six things. How to organise for a local venture, and how to work with other Christians; that each part of the local church complements the others, and that each member's help is essential; the need for each member to have a job in the church, and the fact that God answers prayer: 'The salvation of lost souls should be a constant experience and not an isolated happening.'

In year three, local churches faced the task of implementing those lessons, which were common to many churches throughout the country. Those which had put much into the missions found that they had received out of them much more than names of enquirers. They had received inspiration and stimulation.

All the regional offices planned to remain open for the duration of the third year, although with a small staff (in some cases only one person). Their functions would be to co-ordinate some activities at area level: meetings and missions for clusters of churches.

That left some people with a sinking feeling as they peered further ahead to 1986 and feared that the momentum would slowly grind to a halt. Could not Mission England continue beyond that date in some form? No! said the Bishop of Thetford and Mission England regional chairman for East Anglia (north), the Rt Rev. Timothy Dudley-Smith. 'The task of evangelism is the task of the local churches,' he wrote in the regional bulletin. 'That is the pattern of the New Testament, and it is one we must all work for.'

Perhaps evangelistic committees will spring out of Mission England in some areas, maintaining the breadth of support which existing enabling bodies do not enjoy. Perhaps some of those existing organisations are indeed destined to die and new ones, with their roots in Mission England, will rise to take their place to face new challenges.

But the temptation is always strong to take on more baggage than God wants to give; remember David and Goliath. Or to build bigger structures than he wants us to rely on; remember the tower of Babel. The end result of organising the Holy Spirit out of a job, of institutionalising his spontaneous outpouring, is usually to staunch the flow of living water and to end up marooned on a drifting ice floe. To do nothing at all, however, but to bask on the shore and to soak up the warm glow which lingers from an exceptional summer of mission; to revert to the old patterns of church life, the old half-hearted, half-unbelieving witness to a world of which we are half afraid: that would be to cause the waters to stagnate.

Tom Houston, then Executive Director of the Bible Society in London, had been Chairman of Mission England during its first formative months. When he became President of World Vision International and moved to the USA, he had to relinquish his Mission England role. But for two nights, as he was passing through Britain again, he went to the meetings at Liverpool's Anfield soccer ground. On one of them he came to the microphone.

'The tide has been going out for our country in many respects for a long time. And one of the reasons for that in my estimation,' he said, 'is that we have lived as a nation without any word abroad in the land that there was a God to whom we were responsible and one who loved us and cared. And now that message is coming back in full force through Mission England and the ministry of Dr Billy Graham.

'I believe that the response of the people indicates that the time has come when people will heed that message, the love of God through Jesus Christ.

'I've been travelling in 15 countries since I left here in January, and I have increasing confidence in the good news of Jesus Christ. When the problem in society is polarisation and conflict, where else can you have a message of reconciliation based on both sides receiving forgiveness through the death of another? When the issue is money, where else is there a message where the bottom line is neither wages nor profits, but sharing what God gives? When the root problem is selfishness, where else is there a source of undying love that when people experience it they're ready to love one another as they love themselves? When frustration and a sense of powerlessness is abroad, where else is there a promise of power from above by the Holy Spirit?

'And that's the message that's going out through Mission England and Billy Graham these days. And to me it's an answer to prayer and a turning of the tide. May it be so for His name's sake.'

The Billy Graham missions in England in the summer of 1984 have long since ended, and the soccer grounds they were held in reverberate once again to a very different rendering of *You'll never walk alone*; the third year of the programme is barely under way as this book goes to press.

The next chapter, therefore, begins as you put this book back on the shelf. Even if you do feel a very small one in a very large million...

APPENDIX A

MISSION ENGLAND 1984
SUMMARY OF ATTENDANCE AND ENQUIRERS
AT STADIUM MEETINGS

Dates		Attendance	Enquirers	%
South West Mission: Bristol				
Saturday	12 May	31,012	2,352	7.6
Sunday	13 May	25,127	2,172	8.7
Monday	14 May	30,181	2,642	8.8
Tuesday	15 May	26,544	2,373	8.9
Wednesday	16 May	31,017	2,262	7.3
Thursday	17 May	25,511	1,727	6.8
Friday	18 May	36,504	3,962	10.9
Saturday	19 May	38,112	2,954	7.8
		244,008	20,444	8.4
North East Mission: Sunderland				
Saturday	26 May	16,140	1,253	8.0
Sunday	27 May	10,636	764	7.0
Monday	28 May	10,766	1,559	14.5
Tuesday	29 May	16,838	1,436	8.5
Wednesday	30 May	20,363	1,766	8.7
Thursday	31 May	15,004	1,170	7.8
Friday	1 June	15,318	1,949	13.0
Saturday	2 June	19,032	1,888	10.0
		124,097	11,785	9.5
East Anglia North Mission: Norwich				
Saturday	9 June	17,491	1,303	7.5
Sunday	10 June	18,194	848	4.7
Monday	11 June	14,330	884	6.2
Tuesday	12 June	13,113	667	5.1
		63,128	3,702	5.9

Dates		Attendance	Enquirers	%
Midlands Mission: Birmingham				
Saturday	30 June	31,497	3,053	9.7
Sunday	1 July	29,384	2,739	9.3
Monday	2 July	31,000	2,699	8.7
Tuesday	3 July	33,553	3,154	9.4
Wednesday	4 July	33,986	3,111	9.2
Thursday	5 July	27,915	2,697	9.7
Friday	6 July	39,000	5,034	12.9
Saturday	7 July	30,680	3,694	12.0
		257,015	26,181	10.2
North West Mission: Liverpool				
Saturday	14 July	27,051	3,075	11.4
Sunday	15 July	17,224	1,896	11.0
Monday	16 July	32,111	3,264	10.2
Tuesday	17 July	37,892	3,985	10.5
Wednesday	18 July	35,971	3,957	11.0
Thursday	19 July	32,047	3,649	11.4
Friday	20 July	35,415	4,017	11.3
Saturday	21 July	30,278	3,569	11.8
		247,989	27,412	11.0
East Anglia South: Ipswich				
Tuesday	24 July	16,452	1,404	8.5
Wednesday	25 July	20,032	1,771	8.8
Thursday	26 July	17,343	1,646	9.5
Friday	27 July	18,032	1,345	7.5
Saturday	28 July	18,504	1,292	7.0
		90,363	7,458	8.3
National Totals				
As of 30 July, 1984		1,026,600	96,982	9.4

Note: Of the enquirers, 61 per cent were under 25 years of age.

APPENDIX B
MISSION ENGLAND 1984
CHURCH AND INDIVIDUAL INVOLVEMENT

Region	South West	North East	East Anglia (North)	Midlands	North West	East Anglia (South)	Totals
Number of churches involved	721	352	850	883	1,194	750	4,750
*Number of Christian Life & Witness Classes	56	36	39	93	88	43	355
*Number attending Christian Life & Witness Classes	11,690	4,500	5,240	12,711	10,661	5,178	49,980
**Number of Caring for New Christian Groups	150	77	30	1,746	114	66	2,183
**Number attending Caring for New Christian Courses	7,050	2,940	1,000	2,940	6,380	2,568	22,878
Number of Stewards	700	445	350	821	742	425	3,483
Number of Counsellors	3,907	1,533	1,456	5,802	4,650	2,200	19,548
Number in Choir	2,700	1,802	1,745	2,313	3,700	2,475	14,735
Number in Follow-up Team	500	381	372	520	850	550	3,173
Number of paid staff	4	2	3	5	7	3	24
Number of regular volunteer staff	50	40	40	35	14	4	183

*Christian Life and Witness Classes – a four week course to help Christians understand and share their faith more effectively.
**Caring for New Christian Courses – to help people who will be involved with Bible study groups for newly committed Christians.

APPENDIX C

MISSION ENGLAND COUNCIL OF REFERENCE

Chairman

Lord Tonypandy (Former speaker of the House of Commons)

The Council of Reference

Rt Hon Michael Alison MP
Prof Sir Norman Anderson
Prof Graham Ashworth
Rt Rev Michael Baughen
Rev Dr George Beasley Murray
Sir Cyril Black
Viscount Brentford
Viscountess Brentford
Rev Dr Raymond Brown
Rev David Bubbers
Lord Cameron
Rev Canon Frank Colquhoun
Anthony Cordle Esq
Rev Amos Cresswell
Mrs Jill Dann
Mrs Jean Darnall
Ven John Delight
Rt Rev Timothy Dudley-Smith
Rev Dr Donald English

William Fitch Esq
Rt Rev Goodwin Hudson
Rev Canon Michael Green
Dr Michael Griffiths
Sir Timothy Hoare
Very Rev Brandon Jackson
Rev Gilbert Kirby
Rev Canon Tom Livermore
Dr Brian Mawhinney MP
Rev Dr Alan Redpath
Cliff Richard Esq
Rev Dr John Stott
Rev Canon Harry Sutton
Rt Rev John Taylor
Dr Ann Townsend
Ven Roy Williamson
Major-General Wilson Haffenden
Rt Rev Maurice Wood

Last word

There is no doubt that the three months during which I shared in Mission England were one of the highlights of my entire ministry. The stirring, humbling sight of so many thousands of people coming forward at our meetings, hungry for God and eager to make their commitment to Christ, was one I shall never forget.

And I will always remember that the missions involved a huge number of Christians from many churches, all working and praying together. I have rarely seen a mission so well prepared as this was. I am not talking about a few committees; not even about thousands of churches. But about tens of thousands of Christians all doing something to tell their neighbourhoods the good news of Jesus Christ. I wish all your stories could have been recorded in this book, but only heaven will reveal all the wonderful things which happened when so many people went out in faith and saw God answering their prayers.

I want to express my heartfelt thanks to everyone who was involved; it was much more your mission than it was mine. But of course, it was not really our mission at all; it was God's. He united us in a common task, he gave us strength and spiritual resources beyond our expectation, and he worked among us in ways greater than we could ask or think; to him be the glory.

Now, you face so many new Christians to care for, and new opportunities to proclaim the same gospel. I found people in England very willing to listen and to respond to the simple, biblical message that Christ died for our sins and rose to give us new and everlasting life.

It is my prayer that all who read this book will be challenged to make a fresh commitment to the Lord of the harvest who sends us out to work and witness in fields ripe for reaping. When I was in England I sometimes said that I believed the nation was on the verge of spiritual awakening. I believe that even more now. And then, England could become once more a light shining in the growing darkness which threatens to envelope the world.

It is only by faith in Jesus Christ that we can face the future with hope and confidence. He alone offers the power to conquer the evils which threaten us. He alone offers forgiveness of our sins and the promise of eternal life. We all need all that he has to offer. May we know it for ourselves, and may we help many others discover him too.

Billy Graham